MMPI-A Content Scales

MMPI-A Monograph

MMPI-A Content Scales
Assessing Psychopathology
in Adolescents

Carolyn L. Williams
James N. Butcher
Yossef S. Ben-Porath
John R. Graham

Foreword by Alan E. Kazdin

University of Minnesota Press
Minneapolis • London

Published by the University of Minnesota Press
2037 University Avenue Southeast, Minneapolis, MN 55414
Printed in the United States of America on acid-free paper

Library of Congress Cataloging-in-Publication Data

MMPI-A content scales : assessing psychopathology in adolescents /
    Carolyn L. Williams . . . [et al.].
        p.   cm.—(MMPI-A monograph)
    Includes bibliographical references and index.
    ISBN 0-8166-2144-6 (hc : alk. paper)
    1. Minnesota Multiphasic Personality Inventory for Adolescents.
2. Adolescent psychopathology—Diagnosis. I. Williams, Carolyn L.,
1951– . II. Series.
    [DNLM: 1. MMI—in adolescence.   2. Personality Assessment—in
adolescence.   3. Psychopathology—in adolescence.   WM 145 M6856]
RJ503.7.M56M57   1992
616.89'022—dc20
DNLM/DLC
for Library of Congress   92-3157
                                                                  CIP

Contents

Figures

Tables

Foreword

Among the many goals of assessment is the development of measures of personality and psychopathology across the life span. The diversity of psychological and interpersonal processes, the incomplete charting of these processes, and the impact and course of "normal" development on virtually all facets of psychological functioning are formidable challenges, to say the least. Among the broadly delineated periods of childhood, adolescence, and adulthood, adolescence has endured particular neglect. From the standpoint of assessment, the period of adolescence presents dilemmas. On the one hand, adolescents and adults share some obvious capacities. For example, unlike children, adolescents can comprehend and complete most of the psychological measures expressly designed for adults. This has led naturally to the use of diverse measures for adolescents, albeit measures that were developed for adults. On the other hand, adolescents and adults are obviously quite different, a fact consensually reaffirmed by adolescents and adults on a daily basis. The differences reflect the complex interplay of intrapersonal, interpersonal, and biological processes associated with different phases and stages of development. From the standpoint of scale construction, the differences require consideration of variations in content and scaling of the measures.

The task of developing assessment entails ensuring that the content is relevant to adolescents and collecting normative data to permit interpretation of these content scales. Efforts to accomplish facets of this task have infrequently appeared in the assessment of adolescent personality and psychopathology. The present book provides an exemplary program of work to develop the MMPI for adolescents (MMPI-A) and its content scales.

The development of assessments for adolescents represents one context from which this book might be viewed. Of course, the MMPI has a unique history in psychological assessment and special status of its own. The measure has achieved impact without peer at once representing an approach toward assessment and a measure that has had broad use and impact on diverse areas of application within psychology and public life. The literature that has been spawned by the MMPI and derivative measures is remarkable.

The MMPI-2 represents a restandardization of the original instrument, encompassing a large-scale effort spanning several years. The restandardization effort began explicitly to address the use of the MMPI in relation to adults. At the outset, an experimental effort was undertaken to consider the development of a version of the test for adolescents. The present book charts the development of that measure and the content scales for use with adolescents.

Interest in the use of the MMPI with adolescents can be traced to the initial development of the instrument, with continued empirical efforts through contemporary research. Prior research has not provided a consistent or comprehensive way to use and interpret the test. The development of the MMPI-A is designed to provide the needed conceptual and research bases for such use. The MMPI-A reflects the development of content scales unique to adolescents. Although there is intended overlap in items and scales with the version used with adults (MMPI-2), the goal was to design the measure to reflect the issues and concerns of adolescents. The significance of the book is not only in the content scales that were devised, but also in the weaving of deductive and empirical steps to achieve that end. The stages of scale development and the evolution and survival of content scales through the process are exceptional in their own right.

The authors place the development of the MMPI-A in historical context of the use of the MMPI with adolescents, the problems of the original MMPI and its normative data base for adolescents, and the clear need for a more definitive measure. The development of the MMPI-A is based on the evaluation of more than 2,300 youth involving normative samples of males and females from different geographical regions of the continental United States as well as diverse clinical samples. Scale development, psychometric features, and initial validity evidence based on sample differences and relations of the scales to other standardized measures are systematically detailed.

The authors are modest in their claims for what they have achieved and presented to us in this book. They mark the present book as a beginning effort to develop and establish the MMPI-A. Research on construct validity is a never-ending process; in principle, development and evaluation of a measure are continuous processes. Yet, the authors provide a model for us regarding the means and ends of meticulous assessment work and count as a beginning what many measures have not achieved after years of use. This book will be of keen interest to the large audience of persons interested in the measure itself, as well as those interested in the development of assessment devices more generally.

Alan E. Kazdin

Preface

Of all the developmental periods, adolescence is one of the most challenging for the assessment of psychopathology. This is clearly evident in using the MMPI with adolescents, for it is hard to imagine any other group for whom there is so much controversy and confusion about the use of this instrument. Many idiosyncratic procedures have been developed over the years for interpreting MMPI profiles of adolescents, with no single approach standing out as best. The research base for using the MMPI with adolescents certainly is less extensive than for adults, which likely is a factor in the difficulties of assessing adolescents. However, developmental influences must also be considered as contributory.

Identity formation and the development of abstract reasoning skills are hallmarks of adolescence. Erikson's theory of identity suggests that it is during adolescence that individuals begin to answer the question, "Who am I?" It is understandable that the complex task of identity formation awaits the emergence of abstract reasoning skills, which also occurs during adolescence. This developmental perspective is informative when one considers what is required of individuals completing an MMPI: they must use their true or false responses to MMPI items to provide self-descriptions. It does not seem coincidental that self-report instruments such as the MMPI demonstrate validity with adolescents, but not with younger children at earlier developmental levels. Nor is it difficult to appreciate developmental explanations for the variations between adolescent and adult responses to the MMPI.

Developmental psychologists demonstrate that adolescents, like children, are not miniature adults. Thus, psychological tests used in clinical practice with adults may require greater adaptation than has been past practice for use with adolescents. The adolescent version of the MMPI (MMPI-A), a result of the MMPI Restandardization Project, is the first major effort to improve the instrument for use with adolescents. Most previous attempts to adapt the MMPI for adolescents have been limited to refinements at the norm and scale descriptor levels, to the neglect of item-level or scale-level improvements. MMPI items written for adults and the MMPI standard scales, developed empirically with adult normative and clinical samples, have been used without modifications with adolescents. The MMPI-A, on the other hand, contains adolescent-specific item content, and this monograph details our development of content scales using rational and statistical procedures similar to those used in our work on the adult MMPI-2 (Butcher, Graham, Williams, & Ben-Porath, 1990). The important difference is that our rational approach takes into account developmental issues and our statistical analyses use samples of adolescents.

This monograph begins with a review of past research on use of the MMPI with adolescents. Issues and problems at the item, scale, norm, and descriptor levels are highlighted in Chapter 1, which also summarizes the major interpretive strategies used with the original MMPI with adolescents. Chapter 2 places our work within the context of the MMPI Restandardization Project's development of the MMPI-A. The various settings and samples used in our developmental work are described, including the normative data collection and the clinical sites. Chapter 3 describes the rationale for our scale development steps, which parallel the rational and statistical procedures used in developing the MMPI-2 Content Scales (Butcher et al., 1990). Chapter 4 provides information on the psychometric properties of the MMPI-A Content Scales, including measures of reliability (both internal consistency and test-retest reliability) and the internal validity of our content scales (i.e., the MMPI-A Content Scales' relations with other MMPI measures, such as the standard scales and the Wiggins Content Scales). These psychometric properties are detailed in several samples, both normative and clinical. Chapter 5 examines the validity of our content scales. Empirically derived descriptors are presented for each of the MMPI-A Content Scales—again, from several settings. In Chapter 6, we conclude with an interpretive strategy for the MMPI-A and its content scales, illustrated with case material.

Our work would not have been possible without the support and efforts of more than 2,500 young people and their parents who participated as subjects in our research studies. The young people in our normative samples contributed an average of three hours of their time completing the experimental adolescent form of the MMPI, as well as other MMPI Restandardization Project forms. The young people in our clinical study spent approximately five hours providing us with information about the types of problems they were having. Many of their parents also provided behavioral rating information.

This information was then shared with their treatment staff in order to help formulate treatment plans for the problems they were experiencing. Our clinical subjects and their parents were also aware that they were contributing to the development of an instrument that would be used with other adolescents in trouble.

A number of other psychologists helped supervise our normative data collection, and we are very appreciative of their efforts. W. Grant Dahlstrom and Leona Dahlstrom supervised the data collection for the North Carolina normative subjects. Father Vincent Hevern's volunteered efforts contributed greatly to the successful data collection in New York. Stephen Husband, Michael Snyter, and Marsha Snyter coordinated data collection in Pennsylvania. Robert Archer and Raymont Gordon were responsible for organizing data-collection efforts in Virginia and were assisted by Donna Klinefelter and Rebecca Keever. Dennis Saccuzzo, with the assistance of Konstantinos Kostas, Virginia Anderson, and Charles Freeman, organized the data collection in San Diego. We are also grateful for the efforts of Donna Starr, Virginia Cross, Robin LaDue, and the Muckleshoot Tribal Council for the data collection in Auburn, Washington.

We were fortunate to work with very cooperative schools and districts: Sanford Junior High School (Minneapolis Special School District 1), Thomas Jefferson Senior High School (Bloomington School District 271), Robbinsdale-Armstrong High School (Robbinsdale School District 281), Regis High School in New York City, Roosevelt High School in Kent, Ohio, the Norfolk Public School System in Virginia, the Philadelphia Public School System in Pennsylvania, the Muckleshoot Tribal School, and Chaparral High School, Grossmont High School, and Mount Miguel High School in San Diego. Jerry Tomlinson of the Minneapolis Schools and Roger Sandvick of the Bloomington Schools were especially helpful in their districts.

The treatment staff at the various clinical sites were extraordinarily cooperative, and we are deeply indebted for their contributions to the project. These sites included Fairview Deaconess Hospital, St. Mary's Hospital, Family Networks Day Treatment Centers I and II, and Harrison Secondary School and the School Rehabilitation Center of the Minneapolis Special School District 1. Treatment counselors and schoolteachers spent hours providing ratings for our cases. Individuals we would particularly like to thank for help with the clinical data collection include Nancy Rains, Philip Klees, Lynn Strauss, and Gordon Wrobel.

We were fortunate in having funding in addition to the basic support provided by the University of Minnesota Press for the development of the MMPI-A and its norms. Several grants to Dr. Williams provided for the collection of the clinical data used in our validity analyses. The Rivendell Foundation provided partial funding for data collection for the clinical sample. Multi-Health Systems of Toronto provided the computer software for the Diagnostic Interview for Children and Adolescents (DICA). We are also grateful for the technical assistance of Steven Stein and his staff regarding use of the DICA. Funding awarded to Dr. Williams by the Biomedical Research Support Grant Program, Division of Research Resources, National Institute of Health (BRSG S07 RR 055 448) allowed for the collection and processing of additional measures for the subsample of normative subjects from Robbinsdale-Armstrong High School in the Twin Cities. Considerable research support was provided by the MMPI-2 Workshops, Department of Psychology, University of Minnesota. Research assistant support from the School of Public Health at the University of Minnesota allowed for additional data collection, processing, and analysis. The University of Minnesota Academic Computing Services and Systems also provided grants to Drs. Butcher and Williams for data analyses.

Over the years a number of graduate and undergraduate students volunteered their time or worked as research assistants on various studies. Individuals from the University of Minnesota included Leslie Adler, Ann Bunde, Peggy Elstun, Karen Gayda, Kyunghee Han, Kirsten Hostetler, Laura Keller, Debbie Kopp, Pauline Nguyen, James Poling, Brad Roper, Wendy Slutske, Craig Uchiyama, and Nathan Weed. Pamela Fahey provided excellent skills and many hours in word processing and in checking and double-checking data in the tables. Rebecca Turner subsequently demonstrated similar competence in the completion of this monograph. Liz Anderson assisted with many of the tables, as did Chris Elwell. Kent State students who contributed to this project as research assistants were Leanna Hale, Scott Kieller, Eileen McCully, Denise Shondrick, and Rodney Timbrook. Mary Alice Schumaker provided very useful editorial suggestions. Linda Nelson and Dennis Saccuzzo gave many helpful comments in their reviews for the publisher.

Finally, we are also indebted to the members of the Adolescent MMPI Project Committee for their contributions: Robert Archer, Beverly Kaemmer, and, most notably, the special efforts made by Auke Tellegen.

Chapter 1

Application of the MMPI in the Assessment of Adolescents

*The adolescent stage of life has long seemed to me one of the most fasci-
nating of all themes, more worthy, perhaps, than anything else in the world
of reverence, most inviting study, and in most crying need of a service we
do not yet understand how to render aright.*
G. Stanley Hall (1904, p. xviii)

Almost 50 years after G. Stanley Hall inaugurated the scientific study
of adolescence, Starke Hathaway, one of the authors of the Minnesota
Multiphasic Personality Inventory (MMPI), began his landmark studies on adolescent personality and behavior. Hall (1904) earlier identified the difficulties inherent in studying this developmental period:
"Character and personality are taking form, but everything is plastic
. . . every trait and faculty is liable to exaggeration and excess" (p. xv).
The very nature of adolescence indicated growing, developing, and
changing individuals who had tendencies toward overstatement, a
considerable challenge for personality researchers using a self-report
instrument such as the MMPI. Despite these obstacles, data collected
by Hathaway and his colleague, Elio Monachesi, demonstrated that
the MMPI could measure personality characteristics, as early as in the
ninth grade, that predicted such important problem behaviors as delinquency and dropping out of school at later ages (Hathaway &
Monachesi, 1953, 1957, 1961, 1963; Hathaway, Monachesi, & Young,
1959, 1960; Hathaway, Reynolds, & Monachesi, 1969).

A Historical Perspective

Much of what is known about using the MMPI with adolescents comes
from studies conducted in schools throughout Minnesota shortly after
the inventory's development in the late 1930s and 1940s (Hathaway &
Monachesi, 1953, 1957, 1961, 1963; Hathaway et al., 1959, 1960,
1969). These data provided a basis for the subsequent development of
adolescent norms for the MMPI by Phillip Marks and Peter Briggs (reported in Dahlstrom, Welsh, & Dahlstrom, 1972; Marks, Seeman, &
Haller, 1974). In fact, even during the 1980s, researchers continued to
use the data set collected by Hathaway and Monachesi to develop
"new" MMPI norms for adolescents (Gottesman, Hanson, Kroeker, &

Briggs, 1987). Although the MMPI became one of the most frequently used psychological tests in studies with adolescents (LeUnes,
Evans, Karnei, & Lowry, 1980), MMPI research on young people
lagged behind the wealth of information collected about the use of the
test with adults. Apparently, in spite of G. Stanley Hall's enthusiastic
endorsement of the study of adolescence, research on the use of the
MMPI with adolescents suffered the same marginal status as its parent
field of adolescent psychology, with psychologists and others studying
adolescence much less frequently than other developmental periods
(Kendall & Williams, 1986).

In spite of the passage of considerable time since the collection of
their data, Hathaway and Monachesi's legacy should not be under-
stated. Had others undertaken similar studies, we would now know
much more about adolescent personality in general and the use of the
MMPI with this age range in particular. Their longitudinal study
spanned 13 years and included a representative statewide sample of
11,329 ninth-grade students from 92 schools in 86 communities from
47 of Minnesota's 87 counties. Data collection on the primary sample
began in the spring of 1954. An earlier sample of 4,572 Minneapolis
ninth graders (87% of the school district's enrollment) was collected
during the 1947-1948 school year and was followed up two to four
years later (Hathaway & Monachesi, 1963).

Evidence of the validity of the MMPI's standard scales in school
populations was provided by Hathaway and Monachesi (1963). They
studied relations between the 10 MMPI standard scales (see Table 1-1
for a description of the standard and validity scales) and a number of
demographic and behavioral variables available through school
records, self-reports, and teacher nominations of students most likely
to exhibit delinquent behavior or emotional disturbance. Subsequent
follow-up information was obtained approximately two to four years
after the original MMPI testing and included searches of police and
court records to identify delinquents, as well as interviews with school
personnel about individual students' conduct and adjustment. Hathaway and Monachesi (1963), consistent with their MMPI interpretive
strategy, presented descriptors for MMPI standard scales when they
were the highest scale in the profile. Their high point scales had to
achieve an adult T-score elevation greater than 54 in order to be
studied.

Scale 4 had the greatest number of descriptors associated with clinically relevant outcomes. Scale 4 as the highest point in an adolescent's
profile was related to poor school adjustment and conduct, the highest
delinquency ratings, teacher-predicted delinquency and emotional
problems, being a school dropout, and being from a separated or di-
vorced family. These findings replicated across genders. Scale 8 as the

TABLE 1-1. Original MMPI validity indicators and standard scales

Scale	Abbreviation	Original name	Number of items MMPI/MMPI-A	Description
			Validity indicators	
?	Cs	Cannot Say	Varies on both	Cs is not actually a scale, but simply the number of omitted items in an individual's protocol. There can be many reasons for omitting items, including carelessness, confusion, indecisiveness, defensiveness, or a lack of relevant information or experience for making a meaningful response. Regardless of the reasons for omitting items, a large number of such items can lead to lowered scores on other scales. Traditionally, Cs raw scores greater than 30 on the 566-item MMPI are interpreted as indicating profile invalidity. The number of Cs items can be decreased by encouraging the individual to try to answer previously omitted items.
L	—	Lie	15/14	Items dealing with relatively minor flaws and weaknesses were rationally selected for this validity scale. Individuals deliberately trying to present themselves in a very favorable way often are not willing to admit to even such minor shortcomings. Scores on this scale are related to educational level, intelligence, socioeconomic status, and psychological sophistication.

TABLE 1-1. Original MMPI validity indicators and standard scales (continued)

Scale	Abbreviation	Original name	Number of items MMPI/MMPI-A	Description
			Validity indicators (cont.)	
F	—	Infrequency	64/66	Developed to detect deviant or atypical ways of responding to MMPI items. Its items are those answered in the scored direction by less than 10% of adult normal subjects. Thus, persons endorsing many F Scale items in the scored direction are not responding as most normal people do. High scores on F are associated with elevated clinical scales, especially Scales 6 and 8. F is used as an index of test-taking attitude and for detecting deviant responses that arrive from poor reading or confusion. If one can rule out profile invalidity, the F Scale is a good indicator of degree of psychopathology, with higher scores suggestive of greater pathology.
K	—	Defensiveness	30 on both	Developed as a more subtle and effective index than L to identify attempts to deny psychopathology and present oneself in an overly favorable light. High scores on K were thought to be associated with a defensive approach to the test, whereas low scores were indicative of unusual frankness and self-criticism. Subsequent work on K revealed it to be much more complex. Scores on K are related to clinical defensiveness, but also to educational level and higher socioeconomic status, with better educated and higher socioeconomic-level subjects scoring higher on the scale. In addition, moderate elevations on K can indicate ego strength and psychological resources.

Scale	Abbreviation	Original name	Number of items MMPI/MMPI-A	Description
			Standard scales	
1	Hs	Hypochondriasis	33/32	Developed to identify patients with excessive bodily concern and preoccupation with symptoms of somatic disease. It is the most unidimensional of the standard scales, characterized by the denial of good health and the admission of a variety of physical symptoms.
2	D	Depression	60/57	Developed to assess symptomatic depression that is characterized by poor morale, lack of hope in the future, and a general dissatisfaction with one's life. Item content includes symptoms of subjective depression, lack of energy, somatic complaints, concentration and memory difficulties, lack of self-confidence, and rumination.
3	Hy	Hysteria	60 on both	Developed to identify patients exhibiting a hysterical reaction to stress. Item content includes a feeling of ill health and fatigue, multiple somatic complaints, a need for affection, denial of social anxiety, and a denial of hostile or aggressive impulses or interests.
4	Pd	Psychopathic Deviate	50/49	Developed to identify patients diagnosed as having psychopathic, asocial, or amoral personality disorders. A wide array of problems is contained in its items, including family discord, authority problems, social alienation, and self-alienation, as well as items suggesting self-confidence and exhibitionism.

TABLE 1-1. Original MMPI validity indicators and standard scales (continued)

Scale	Abbreviation	Original name	Number of items MMPI/MMPI-A	Description
			Standard scales (cont.)	
5	Mf	Masculinity-Femininity	60/44	Developed using primarily men to identify "sexual inversion." The test authors were unsuccessful in developing a corresponding scale for women, resulting in the standard practice of using Scale 5 for both genders. Most of its items are keyed in the same direction for both genders, although five items dealing with frankly sexual material are keyed in opposite directions for men and women. Many of its items are not sexual in nature and cover a diversity of topics, including interests in work, hobbies, worries, fears, sensitivities, social activities, religious preferences, and family relationships.
6	Pa	Paranoia	40 on both	Developed to identify patients judged to have paranoid symptoms (i.e., ideas of reference, feelings of persecution, grandiose self-concepts, suspiciousness, excessive sensitivity, and rigid opinions and attitudes). Some of the items deal with frankly psychotic behaviors, although other items cover diverse topics such as sensitivity, cynicism, asocial behavior, excessive moral virtue, rigidity, and complaints about other people.
7	Pt	Psychasthenia	48 on both	Developed to identify patients diagnosed with psychasthenia, a diagnostic label not in current use (obsessive compulsive disorder probably is the closest modern equivalent). Many of its items deal with uncontrollable or obsessive thoughts, feelings of fear and/or anxiety, self-doubts, physical complaints, and concentration difficulties.

Scale	Abbreviation	Original name	Number of items MMPI/MMPI-A	Description
			Standard scales (cont.)	
8	Sc	Schizophrenia	78/72	Developed to identify patients diagnosed as schizophrenic. Its items cover a wide array of behaviors, including frankly psychotic symptoms such as bizarre mentation, perceptual distortions, delusions of persecution, and hallucinations. Other content includes social alienation, poor family relations, sexual concerns, difficulty in impulse control and concentration, and fears, worries, and dissatisfaction.
9	Ma	Hypomania	46 on both	Developed to identify psychiatric patients manifesting hypomanic symptoms (i.e., elevated mood, accelerated speech and motor activity, irritability, flight of ideas, and brief periods of depression). Items deal with activity level, excitability, as well as a denial of social anxiety, exaggeration of self-worth and abilities, and impatience and irritability toward others.
0	Si	Social Introversion	70/62	Developed later than the other standard scales, it was designed to measure a person's tendency to withdraw from social contacts and responsibilities. Items include feelings of inferiority and personal discomfort, discomfort around others, dislike of social groups, oversensitivity, distrust of others, and a number of somatic complaints.

Note: The above information refers to the original MMPI, not the MMPI-2. Unless otherwise noted, any reference to the MMPI in this monograph refers to the original instrument, not the MMPI-2 or MMPI-A.

highest point also was associated with acting-out behaviors, as well as limited intellectual ability and poor academic performance in both genders.

Hathaway and Monachesi (1953, 1963) classified several of the standard scales as having an excitatory or inhibitory association with delinquency. The excitatory scales demonstrated increasing delinquency rates with increasing T scores, and the inhibitory scales demonstrated the reverse relationship. As expected, Scale 4 was a strong excitatory scale. Scales 6 and 8 showed excitatory features as well. The more neurotically based scales (i.e., Scales 2, 3, 5, 7, and 0) were predictive of lower delinquency rates. When both inhibitory and excitatory scales were elevated in a given profile, Hathaway and Monachesi (1963) reported the excitatory scales exerted a stronger effect.

These results with delinquent boys were replicated with nondelinquent boys who had been rated as highly aggressive using a peer nomination technique (Butcher, 1965). Highly aggressive boys were found to have generally high scores on Scales 4, 8, and 9. Boys with low aggression were found to have high scores on Scales 1, 2, 3, 7, 8, and 0. This study demonstrated the effectiveness of the MMPI standard scales in differentiating boys in a regular school setting who were rated according to level of aggression.

It is interesting to note the similarities between Hathaway and Monachesi's (1963) descriptions of the excitatory/inhibitory nature of the MMPI scales and subsequent work using other instruments on undercontrolled/overcontrolled behavioral syndromes in children and adolescents. Achenbach and Edelbrock (1978), reviewing factor-analytic studies of several behavior rating scales in diverse samples of disturbed children, described these two broadband syndromes. Undercontrolled syndromes included problems with aggression, acting out, conduct disorders, or externalizing problems similar to those suggested by the MMPI excitatory scales. Overcontrolled syndromes included inhibited or shy-anxious behavior, or internalizing problems similar to those suggested by the inhibitory MMPI scales. This similarity of the excitatory/inhibitory aspects of the MMPI standard scales to the robust finding of the undercontrolled/overcontrolled dimensions underlying behavior rating scales is suggestive of the validity of the MMPI scales as measures of psychopathology in adolescents.

High point scores on Scales 1, 2, and 3 were rare in Hathaway and Monachesi's large general adolescent sample (e.g., only 89 boys and 21 girls out of 10,104 valid profiles were classified as high point on Scale 1). These inhibitory MMPI scales also were associated with fewer clinically relevant descriptors. This more likely reflected the lack of these variables in the pool of potential descriptors or criterion measures, rather than limited validity for these scales. For example, there were no measures of somatic complaints (frequently found to be related to Scales 1, 2, 3, 7, and 0) among Hathaway and Monachesi's criterion measures.

For more than 25 years, Hathaway and Monachesi's study provided the only source of MMPI scale descriptors for an adolescent population. The only extensive MMPI study of adolescents in clinical settings during that period (i.e., Marks et al., 1974) focused on the code-type approach and did not examine the validity of the MMPI standard scales with its sample of 834 outpatients. Archer, Gordon, Giannetti, and Singles (1988), studying 75 adolescent psychiatric inpatients, provided some support for the validity of MMPI Scales 2, 3, 4, 8, and 9 as high point codes. However, it was not until 1989 that another large adolescent clinical sample of more than 800 adolescents (12-18 years old) was collected to examine the validity of and to derive descriptors for the MMPI standard scales (Williams & Butcher, 1989a). Prior to Williams and Butcher's (1989a) work, scale descriptors from studies with adults (e.g., Graham, 1977, 1987; Greene, 1980) were one method used to interpret MMPI scale elevations for adolescents, based on the assumption that findings from studies of adults should generalize to adolescents. Williams and Butcher (1989a) were able to demonstrate support for this assumption for several of the MMPI standard scales. Scales 1, 2, 3, 4, 8, 9, and 0 had several descriptors consistent with research on adults. There was also some support for the validity of Scale 6 in boys and Scale 7 in girls. The excitatory/inhibitory dimension of the MMPI scales was partially replicated by Williams and Butcher (1989a). Clinically relevant descriptors for Scale 5 remained notably absent.

The import of Hathaway and Monachesi's work goes beyond their contributions to MMPI scale validity and normative data. They were particularly fascinated with the differences in personality among adults and adolescents, as measured by the MMPI. Like G. Stanley Hall, they saw adolescence as a "time often marked by rapid shifts in personality" (Hathaway & Monachesi, 1963, p. viii). Therefore, their research had two main purposes: to provide an estimate of the predictive power of the MMPI administered to ninth-grade adolescents, but also to examine the extent of personality changes from ninth to twelfth grades. They were encouraged by their findings from subjects who completed the MMPI in both grades that the majority of adolescents who scored high on Scale 4 in the ninth grade had different MMPI configurations by the twelfth grade. They suggested that the MMPI provided evidence "that adolescents are flexible and may be helped. . . . it is encouraging to find that so many of them do change" (p. 70).

On the other hand, some of Hathaway and Monachesi's (1963) interpretations of their MMPI findings were consistent with Hall's (1904) storm and stress model of adolescence. For example, one of the clearest differences they found among adult and adolescent MMPI profiles was the greater number of no-high-point profiles among adults. They had defined no-high-point profiles as those with no scales with an adult T score greater than 54. Hathaway and Monachesi (1963) suggested, "To the degree that such profiles are indicative of normal personality, then normal personality is much more frequent among adults than among adolescents" (p. 39). Subsequent research did not support this definition of normal personality. However, Hathaway and Monachesi's work documented other meaningful MMPI differences in adult and adolescent responding that were important to consider. These differences occurred in three main areas: item endorsements, scale elevations, and code types (Williams, 1986).

Differences between Adult and Adolescent MMPI Responses

Item Endorsements

Differences between adult and adolescent responses to the MMPI are apparent at the item level. Tables 1-2 and 1-3 list the MMPI items on which the largest differences in frequency of the response "true" occurred among adults and adolescents in the Hathaway and Monachesi (1963) data. Scale membership of the items is also provided in these tables, indicating that all the validity and standard scales contain some of these items that show adult/adolescent response differences. Table 1-2 presents a rank-order list of the items that most differentiated boys and men, along with corresponding endorsement frequencies of these items among girls and women. The same information is presented in Table 1-3 for girls and women, with comparison information on boys and men. We agree with Hathaway and Monachesi's interpretation of these differences as reflective of developmental issues.

The first item on the list for boys in Table 1-2, "I am neither gaining nor losing weight," does not appear in Table 1-3 for girls. Ninth-grade boys are in the adolescent growth spurt and therefore more likely to report fluctuations in their weight than are men. Girls tend to be two years ahead of boys in their adolescent growth spurt (Tanner, 1971), and thus do not differ from women on this item (Williams, 1986). Other developmental issues are apparent in item endorsement frequencies. Boys and girls react against familial and societal controls

TABLE 1-2. Item-endorsement percentage differences of 25 points or more in "true" responses for men and boys compared with those of women and girls in the Hathaway and Monachesi sample (1963) [1]

Item (Scale membership)	Men			Women		
	Adults (n = 226)	Adolescents (n = 100)	Difference	Adults (n = 315)	Adolescents (n = 100)	Difference
I am neither gaining nor losing weight. (1, 2, 4)	84	26	58	74	54	20
My relatives are nearly all in sympathy with me. (4)	65	18	47	73	22	51
Sometimes at elections I vote for men about whom I know very little. (L)	62	18	44	62	23	39
I would like to hunt lions in Africa.	20	63	43	22	24	2
I like poetry. (5)	59	17	42	87	44	43
I worry over money and business. (K, 8)	53	15	38	58	16	42
I like to attend lectures on serious subjects.	62	28	34	57	31	26
I never worry about my looks. (9)	52	19	33	42	7	35
I would like to be an auto racer.	17	50	33	1	11	10
Someone has been trying to influence my mind. (F, 6)	40	8	32	37	3	34
The one to whom I was most attached and whom I most admired as a child was a woman. (Mother, sister, aunt, or other woman.)	85	54	31	64	79	15
I would like to wear expensive clothes.	72	41	31	97	68	29
I have been quite independent and free from family rule. (4)	70	39	31	67	30	37
I have had periods in which I lost sleep over worry.	54	24	30	68	32	36
I prefer work which requires close attention, to work which allows me to be careless.	83	53	30	76	58	18
I enjoy reading love stories. (5)	47	17	30	73	87	14
I go to church almost every week. (2)	45	75	30	56	90	34
I like to read newspaper editorials.	73	44	29	76	49	27
I could be happy living all alone in a cabin in the woods or mountains.	21	50	29	14	24	10

TABLE 1-2. Item-endorsement percentage differences of 25 points or more in "true" responses for men and boys compared with those of women and girls in the Hathaway and Monachesi sample (1963)[1] (continued)

Item (Scale membership)	Men			Women		
	Adults (n = 226)	Adolescents (n = 100)	Difference	Adults (n = 315)	Adolescents (n = 100)	Difference
At times I feel like picking a fist fight with someone. (2)	24	53	29	17	22	5
I tend to be on my guard with people who are somewhat more friendly than I had expected. (6)	78	49	29	69	49	20
I have often met people who were supposed to be experts who were no better than I. (K)	71	43	28	56	36	20
I am entirely self-confident. (5)	62	34	28	41	20	21
I dream frequently about things that are best kept to myself. (2, 8)	25	52	27	25	48	23
Children should be taught all the main facts of sex. (F)	91	64	27	94	80	14
It is safer to trust nobody. (3)	46	20	26	40	12	28
I think I would like the work of a building contractor. (5)	31	57	26	9	7	2
I like movie love scenes.	54	28	26	81	77	4
I like to read about history.	78	53	25	64	38	26
It makes me nervous to have to wait.	53	28	25	65	46	19
Bad words, often terrible words, come into my mind and I cannot get rid of them. (7)	16	41	25	14	28	14
I often think, "I wish I were a child again." (K, 0)	49	24	25	44	20	24

[1]Reproduced by permission from Hathaway and Monachesi (1963, pp. 126-127).

TABLE 1-3. Item-endorsement percentage differences of 25 points or more in "true" responses for women and girls compared with those of men and boys in the Hathaway and Monachesi sample (1963)[1]

Item (Scale membership)	Women			Men		
	Adults (n = 315)	Adolescents (n = 100)	Difference	Adults (n = 226)	Adolescents (n = 100)	Difference
My relatives are nearly all in sympathy with me. (4)	73	22	51	65	18	47
I would like to be a private secretary.	21	72	51	13	13	0
Usually I would prefer to work with women.	6	54	48	17	15	2
I like poetry. (5)	87	44	43	59	17	42
I worry over money and business. (K, 8)	58	16	42	53	15	38
I feel that it is certainly best to keep my mouth shut when I'm in trouble. (3, 5)	82	40	42	72	56	16
I have very few fears compared to my friends. (4)	74	32	42	73	56	17
It does not bother me that I am not better looking. (5, 0)	83	42	41	89	69	20
When I get bored I like to stir up some excitement. (9)	43	83	40	50	73	23
Dirt frightens or disgusts me.	61	21	40	34	13	21
Sometimes at elections I vote for men about whom I know very little. (L)	62	23	39	62	18	44
I have been quite independent and free from family rule. (4)	67	30	37	70	39	31
I have had periods in which I lost sleep over worry.	68	32	36	54	24	30
I practically never blush.	55	20	35	60	46	14
I never worry about my looks. (9)	42	7	35	52	19	33
I think I would like the work of a dressmaker.	15	50	35	2	3	1
Once in a while I feel hate toward members of my family whom I usually love. (5, 8)	26	60	34	23	46	23
I like to read newspaper articles on crime. (3)	30	64	34	50	65	15
I go to church almost every week. (2)	56	90	34	45	75	30
I have no patience with people who believe there is only one true religion.	53	19	34	44	18	26

TABLE 1-3. Item-endorsement percentage differences of 25 points or more in "true" responses for women and girls compared with those of men and boys in the Hathaway and Monachesi sample (1963)[1] (continued)

Item (Scale membership)	Women			Men		
	Adults (n = 315)	Adolescents (n = 100)	Difference	Adults (n = 226)	Adolescents (n = 100)	Difference
Someone has been trying to influence my mind. (F, 6)	37	3	34	40	8	32
I enjoy detective or mystery stories. (3)	47	78	31	70	79	9
I like to flirt. (2, 0)	24	55	31	34	48	14
I have been inspired to a program of life based on duty which I have since carefully followed. (9)	50	19	31	42	28	14
I daydream very little. (5)	66	37	29	73	66	7
I would like to wear expensive clothes.	97	68	29	72	41	31
I like to go to parties and other affairs where there is lots of loud fun. (5, 0)	39	67	28	60	75	15
Once a week or oftener I become very excited. (7, 8, 9)	17	45	28	10	28	18
I have no fear of water.	49	77	28	70	79	9
At times I have worn myself out by undertaking too much.	74	46	28	57	45	12
I like tall women.	72	44	28	37	16	21
It is safer to trust nobody. (3)	40	12	28	46	20	26
I usually "lay my cards on the table" with people that I am trying to correct or improve.	74	47	27	80	62	18
I am always disgusted with the law when a criminal is freed through the arguments of a smart lawyer. (3, 4, 9)	86	59	27	77	61	16
What others think of me does not bother me. (K, 3, 4)	48	21	27	60	53	7
I like adventure stories better than romantic stories.	54	27	27	78	88	10
I would like to be a nurse. (5)	28	55	27	6	1	5
I like to read newspaper editorials.	76	49	27	73	44	29
I am inclined to take things hard. (7)	57	30	27	38	16	22
I like to attend lectures on serious subjects.	57	31	26	62	28	34

TABLE 1-3. Item-endorsement percentage differences of 25 points or more in "true" responses for women and girls compared with those of men and boys in the Hathaway and Monachesi sample (1963)[1] (continued)

Item (Scale membership)	Women			Men		
	Adults (n = 315)	Adolescents (n = 100)	Difference	Adults (n = 226)	Adolescents (n = 100)	Difference
I shrink from facing a crisis or difficulty. (0)	13	39	26	30	14	16
I find it hard to set aside a task that I have undertaken, even for a short time. (K)	65	39	26	67	44	23
I like to read about history.	64	38	26	78	53	25
I am often afraid that I am going to blush.	28	53	25	19	32	13
One or more members of my family is very nervous.	54	29	25	42	29	13
I should like to belong to several clubs or lodges. (5, 0)	43	68	25	54	50	4
I have met problems so full of possibilities that I have been unable to make up my mind about them. (9)	49	74	25	57	61	4
I wish I were not bothered by thoughts about sex. (5, 8)	11	36	25	22	45	23

[1]Reproduced by permission from Hathaway and Monachesi (1963, pp. 128-129).

more than do adults, perhaps in keeping with their growing need for autonomy. They are freer from such adult worries and responsibilities as money and business, yet report worrying about their looks. They have more interests in adventure (e.g., consider boys' greater desire to hunt lions in Africa). Girls and women differ more in item endorsements than do boys and men. Some of these differences relate to gender roles, with girls endorsing more stereotypically feminine vocation items and preferring to flirt more than women. More than half the girls, but only 6% of the women, report they prefer to work with women.

Tables 1-4 and 1-5 present a similar analysis of item endorsement differences among adults and adolescents for the contemporary MMPI Restandardization Project normative subjects, ages 14 to 18 years (Chapter 2 provides a description of the Restandardization Project and its samples). One finding replicating across time and the two samples is that girls' responses continue to differ more from women's than do boys' responses from men's (Tables 1-3, 1-5). However, younger girls' greater preference for stereotypically feminine vocation interests apparent in the earlier samples did not replicate in the contemporary samples. Girls in the 1940s and 1950s were more likely than women of that time period to want to be private secretaries, nurses, or dressmakers (Table 1-3). The adolescent girls also expressed a greater desire to work with women than did the adult women. These differences in girls' and women's interests did not appear in the contemporary samples (Table 1-5). The differences between the earlier and contemporary samples could be due to changes in attitudes over time, although the differences in the ages of subjects in the two adolescent samples also are possible explanations (i.e., Hathaway & Monachesi's subjects were all in the ninth grade, whereas 66% of the contemporary subjects came from tenth to twelfth grades). However, when we reran the item analyses using only the ninth-grade girls from the normative sample, the younger, contemporary girls did not endorse the stereotypically feminine vocation items differently from contemporary women, as did adolescent girls in the 1940s and 1950s. This suggests that the differences reflect an actual attitude shift in girls' vocational preferences, rather than an artifact of age differences between the earlier and later normative samples.

Adolescents' greater interest in excitement and loud fun, along with their greater disinterest in intellectual pursuits (science, history), relative to adults, is evident in Tables 1-4 and 1-5. Evidence of their greater willingness to report emotionality can also be seen (e.g., see the item "At times I feel like picking a fist fight with someone" in Table 1-4, or "At times I have fits of laughing and crying that I cannot control" in Table 1-5). Some of the differences in adult and adolescent

TABLE 1-4. Item-endorsement percentage differences of 25 points or more in "true" responses for men and boys compared with those of women and girls in the MMPI Restandardization Project sample

Item (Scale membership)	Men			Women		
	Adults ($n = 1,138$)	Adolescents ($n = 805$)	Difference	Adults ($n = 1,462$)	Adolescents ($n = 815$)	Difference
I dream frequently about things that are best kept to myself. (2, 8)*	28	63	35	27	65	38
I wake up fresh and rested most mornings. (1, 3, 7)	69	35	34	66	29	37
I have very few quarrels with members of my family. (K, 4)	79	46	33	78	38	40
I like to read newspaper editorials.*	67	34	33	64	36	28
I feel that I have often been punished without cause. (6, 8, 9)	9	42	33	11	46	35
At times I feel like picking a fist fight with someone. (2)*	16	48	32	8	38	30
Sometimes in elections I vote for people about whom I know very little. (L)*	70	39	31	75	39	36
I like to go to parties and other affairs where there is lots of loud fun. (5, 0)	45	75	30	39	80	41
When I get bored I like to stir up some excitement. (9)	43	73	30	44	80	36
I have strange and peculiar thoughts. (7, 8)	15	45	30	10	46	36
The future is too uncertain for a person to make serious plans.	12	42	30	13	40	27
Often I cross the street in order not to meet someone I see. (7)	9	39	30	11	37	26
I think I would like the kind of work a forest ranger does. (5)	62	33	29	39	22	17
At times I feel like smashing things. (K, 2)	39	68	29	38	70	32
My parents and family find more fault with me than they should. (F, 4)	11	40	29	14	43	29
Bad words, often terrible words, come into my mind and I cannot get rid of them. (7)*	10	39	29	8	39	31
I am bothered by people outside, on the streets, in stores, etc., watching me.	10	39	29	14	47	33

TABLE 1-4. Item-endorsement percentage differences of 25 points or more in "true" responses for men and boys compared with those of women and girls in the MMPI Restandardization Project sample (continued)

Item (Scale membership)	Men			Women		
	Adults (n = 1,138)	Adolescents (n = 805)	Difference	Adults (n = 1,462)	Adolescents (n = 815)	Difference
It does not bother me that I am not better looking. (5, 0)	77	49	28	59	38	21
I like collecting flowers or growing house plants. (5)	43	15	28	79	43	36
Once in a while I feel hate toward members of my family whom I usually love. (5, 8)	32	60	28	44	72	28
I like to keep people guessing what I'm going to do next.	29	57	28	24	53	29
I do many things which I regret afterwards (I regret things more or more often than others seem to). (4, 7)	19	47	28	22	46	24
I like to attend lectures on serious subjects.	66	39	27	65	40	25
I have often felt that strangers were looking at me critically. (5, 0)	24	51	27	25	65	40
I am so touchy on some subjects that I can't talk about them. (8)	21	48	27	28	54	26
At times I have a strong urge to do something harmful or shocking. (8, 9)	19	46	27	16	53	37
Often, even though everything is going fine for me, I feel that I don't care about anything.	16	43	27	17	51	34
I can easily make other people afraid of me, and sometimes do for the fun of it. (F)	8	35	27	5	22	17
I like to read about science.	80	54	26	56	36	20
I think most people would lie to get ahead. (3, 6)	51	77	26	44	70	26
When I take a new job, I like to find out who it is important to be nice to. (5)	38	64	26	29	57	28

TABLE 1-4. Item-endorsement percentage differences of 25 points or more in "true" responses for men and boys compared with those of women and girls in the MMPI Restandardization Project sample (continued)

Item (Scale membership)	Men			Women		
	Adults (n = 1,138)	Adolescents (n = 805)	Difference	Adults (n = 1,462)	Adolescents (n = 815)	Difference
Some people are so bossy that I feel like doing the opposite of what they request, even though I know they are right. (3, 6, 9)	37	63	26	45	79	34
Sometimes everything makes me want to laugh. (6, 7)	31	57	26	34	70	36
I have often found people jealous of my good ideas, just because they had not thought of them first. (0)	20	46	26	17	45	28
I am sure I am being talked about. (4, 6)	18	44	26	17	50	33
I feel hungry almost all the time.	14	40	26	16	39	23
Most nights I go to sleep without thoughts or ideas bothering me. (2, 7)	77	52	25	73	44	29
I like to read about history.*	77	52	25	68	39	29
I like tall women.	72	47	25	60	27	33
If I could get into a movie without paying and be sure I was not seen I would probably do it. (L)	41	66	25	30	62	32
It bothers me to have someone watch me at work even though I know I can do it well.	39	64	25	54	73	19
If several people find themselves in trouble, the best thing for them to do is to agree upon a story and stick to it. (9)	27	52	25	19	50	31
When people do me a wrong, I feel I should pay them back if I can, just for the principle of the thing. (5)	27	52	25	14	34	20
I often think, "I wish I were a child again." (K, 0)*	23	48	25	21	54	33
Parts of my body often have feelings like burning, tingling, crawling, or like "going to sleep." (1)	19	44	25	25	59	34

*Item also shows adult/adolescent differences in the Hathaway and Monachesi (1963) study.

TABLE 1-5. Item endorsement percentage differences of 25 points or more in "true" responses for women and girls compared with those of men and boys in the MMPI Restandardization Project sample

Item (Scale membership)	Women			Men		
	Adults (n = 1,462)	Adolescents (n = 815)	Difference	Adults (n = 1,138)	Adolescents (n = 805)	Difference
At times I have fits of laughing and crying that I cannot control. (6, 7, 8, 9)	18	64	46	6	30	24
I like to go to parties and other affairs where there is lots of loud fun. (5, 0)*	39	80	41	45	75	30
I have very few quarrels with members of my family. (K, 4)	78	38	40	79	46	33
I have often felt that strangers were looking at me critically. (5, 0)	25	65	40	24	51	27
I have periods of such great restlessness that I cannot sit long in a chair. (3, 7, 8, 9)	24	63	39	30	50	20
I dream frequently about things that are best kept to myself. (2, 8)	27	65	38	28	63	35
I wake up fresh and rested most mornings. (1, 3, 7)	66	29	37	69	35	34
At times I have a strong urge to do something harmful or shocking. (8, 9)	16	53	37	19	46	27
I like collecting flowers or growing house plants. (5)	79	43	36	43	15	28
Sometimes in elections I vote for people about whom I know very little. (L)*	75	39	36	70	39	31
When I get bored I like to stir up some excitement. (9)*	44	80	36	43	73	30
Sometimes everything makes me want to laugh. (6, 7)	34	70	36	31	57	26
I have strange and peculiar thoughts. (7, 8)	10	46	36	15	45	30

TABLE 1-5. Item endorsement percentage differences of 25 points or more in "true" responses for women and girls compared with those of men and boys in the MMPI Restandardization Project sample (continued)

Item (Scale membership)	Women			Men		
	Adults (n = 1,462)	Adolescents (n = 815)	Difference	Adults (n = 1,138)	Adolescents (n = 805)	Difference
I feel that I have often been punished without cause. (6, 8, 9)	11	46	35	9	42	33
Some people are so bossy that I feel like doing the opposite of what they request, even though I know they are right. (3, 6, 9)	45	79	34	37	63	26
Parts of my body often have feelings like burning, tingling, crawling, or like "going to sleep." (1)	25	59	34	19	44	25
Often, even though everything is going fine for me, I feel that I don't care about anything.	17	51	34	16	43	27
Most anytime I would rather sit and daydream than do anything else. (F, 8)	12	46	34	12	36	24
I like tall women.*	60	27	33	72	47	25
I often wonder what hidden reason another person may have for doing something nice for me. (3)	25	58	33	29	53	24
I often think, "I wish I were a child again." (K, 0)	21	54	33	23	48	25
I am sure I am being talked about. (4, 6)	17	50	33	18	44	26
I am bothered by people outside, on the streets, in stores, etc., watching me.	14	47	33	10	39	29
At times I feel like smashing things. (K, 2)	38	70	32	39	68	29
If I could get into a movie without paying and be sure I was not seen I would probably do it. (L)	30	62	32	41	66	25
I often feel as if things are not real. (8)	9	41	32	8	32	24

TABLE 1-5. Item endorsement percentage differences of 25 points or more in "true" responses for women and girls compared with those of men and boys in the MMPI Restandardization Project sample (continued)

	Women			Men		
Item (Scale membership)	Adults (n = 1,462)	Adolescents (n = 815)	Difference	Adults (n = 1,138)	Adolescents (n = 805)	Difference
At times I think I am no good at all.	25	56	31	20	35	15
If several people find themselves in trouble, the best thing for them to do is to agree upon a story and stick to it. (9)	19	50	31	27	52	25
Bad words, often terrible words, come into my mind and I cannot get rid of them. (7)	8	39	31	10	39	29
Once a week or oftener I become very excited. (7, 8, 9)*	35	65	30	35	55	20
I have had very peculiar and strange experiences. (4, 8, 0)	18	48	30	24	45	21
I have often been frightened in the middle of the night.	18	48	30	7	31	24
At times I feel like picking a fist fight with someone. (2)	8	38	30	16	48	32
Most nights I go to sleep without thoughts or ideas bothering me. (2, 7)	73	44	29	77	52	25
I like to read about history.*	68	39	29	77	52	25
At times I have very much wanted to leave home. (4, 8, 9)	41	70	29	32	47	15
I like to keep people guessing what I'm going to do next.	24	53	29	29	57	28
My parents and family find more fault with me than they should. (F, 4)	14	43	29	11	40	29
No one seems to understand me. (4, 6, 8)	9	38	29	9	26	17
I like to read newspaper editorials. *	64	36	28	67	34	33
Once in a while I feel hate toward members of my family whom I usually love. (5, 8)*	44	72	28	32	60	28
When I take a new job, I like to find out who it is important to be nice to. (5)	29	57	28	38	64	26

TABLE 1-5. Item endorsement percentage differences of 25 points or more in "true" responses for women and girls compared with those of men and boys in the MMPI Restandardization Project sample (continued)

Item (Scale membership)	Women			Men		
	Adults ($n = 1{,}462$)	Adolescents ($n = 815$)	Difference	Adults ($n = 1{,}138$)	Adolescents ($n = 805$)	Difference
I often have serious disagreements with people who are close to me. (F, 4, 6, 8)	24	52	28	23	47	24
I have often found people jealous of my good ideas, just because they had not thought of them first. (0)	17	45	28	20	46	26
I often feel guilty because I pretend to feel more sorry about something than I really do.	15	43	28	12	34	22
I hear strange things when I am alone. (8)	7	35	28	4	24	20
Once in a while I think of things too bad to talk about. (6, 7, 8, L)	40	67	27	45	62	17
Sometimes without any reason or even when things are going wrong I feel excitedly happy, "on top of the world." (2, 4)	40	67	27	37	56	19
Most people will use somewhat unfair means to get ahead in life. (4, 8)	38	65	27	43	66	23
I think I would like the work of a librarian. (5)	38	11	27	20	7	13
I have a daydream life about which I do not tell other people.	18	45	27	18	37	19
I wish I were not bothered by thoughts about sex. (5, 8)*	14	41	27	21	36	15
The future is too uncertain for a person to make serious plans.	13	40	27	12	42	30
I daydream very little. (5)*	54	28	26	50	39	11
I think most people would lie to get ahead. (3, 6)	44	70	26	51	77	26
I am so touchy on some subjects that I can't talk about them. (8)	28	54	26	21	48	27

TABLE 1-5. Item endorsement percentage differences of 25 points or more in "true" responses for women and girls compared with those of men and boys in the MMPI Restandardization Project sample (continued)

Item (Scale membership)	Women			Men		
	Adults (n = 1,462)	Adolescents (n = 815)	Difference	Adults (n = 1,138)	Adolescents (n = 805)	Difference
I cannot keep my mind on one thing. (8)	15	41	26	15	38	23
Often I cross the street in order not to meet someone I see. (7)	11	37	26	9	39	30
I like to attend lectures on serious subjects.*	65	40	25	66	39	27
If I were an artist I would like to draw flowers. (5)	64	39	25	31	19	12
I do not always tell the truth. (L)	56	81	25	63	80	17
I think a great many people exaggerate their misfortunes in order to gain the sympathy and help of others. (K, 3)	56	81	25	61	79	18
I have met problems so full of possibilities that I have been unable to make up my mind about them. (9)*	53	78	25	50	61	11
I have no fear of water.*	51	76	25	67	75	8
There are certain people whom I dislike so much that I am inwardly pleased when they are catching it for something they have done.	45	70	25	53	69	16
I certainly feel useless at times. (2, 7, K)	38	63	25	34	46	12
Sometimes I am sure that other people can tell what I am thinking.	34	59	25	32	48	16

TABLE 1-5. Item endorsement percentage differences of 25 points or more in "true" responses for women and girls compared with those of men and boys in the MMPI Restandardization Project sample (continued)

Item (Scale membership)	Women			Men		
	Adults (n = 1,462)	Adolescents (n = 815)	Difference	Adults (n = 1,138)	Adolescents (n = 805)	Difference
I have often lost out on things because I couldn't make up my mind soon enough. (3, 0)	30	55	25	32	52	20
Sometimes some unimportant thought will run through my mind and bother me for days. (7, 0)	30	55	25	23	45	22
My way of doing things is apt to be misunderstood by others. (4)	28	53	25	34	54	20
My conduct is largely controlled by the behavior of those around me. (4, 8, 9)	26	51	25	30	49	19

*Item also shows adult/adolescent differences in the Hathaway and Monachesi (1963) study.

Figure 1-1
Boys Normative Sample Plotted on Three Different Norms

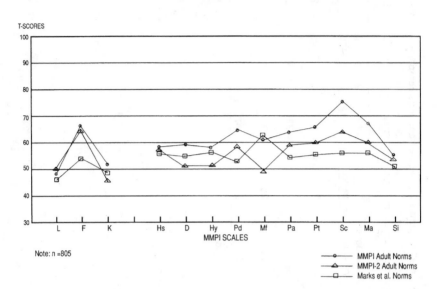

Note: n =805

—○— MMPI Adult Norms
—△— MMPI-2 Adult Norms
—□— Marks et al. Norms

responses to the MMPI can be observed on items assessing more pathological problems. For example, 45% of normative boys and 46% of normative girls admit to having "strange and peculiar thoughts," compared with only 15% of normative men and 10% of normative women (Table 1-4). Likewise, adolescents are more likely to report urges to do harmful or shocking things, ideas of reference, feelings of unreality, and peculiar and strange experiences (Tables 1-4 and 1-5). Scales developed for adults that include these items more frequently endorsed by normal adolescents may have lower validity with adolescents than with adults.

Scale Elevations

MMPI profiles of adults and adolescents frequently differ on the dimension of scale elevation. It has been demonstrated in numerous studies that adolescents' profiles plotted on adult norms achieve higher elevations than do adult profiles. Figure 1-1 for boys and Figure 1-2 for girls illustrate this finding with the adolescent normative sample (ages 14-18 years) from the MMPI Restandardization Project.

Figure 1-2
Girls Normative Sample Plotted on Three Different Norms

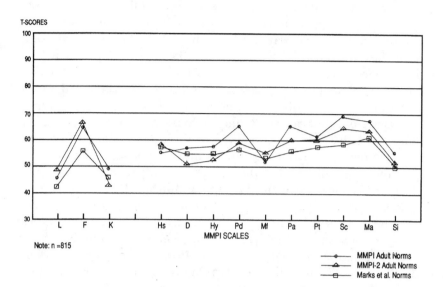

Note: n =815

———○——— MMPI Adult Norms
———△——— MMPI-2 Adult Norms
———▫——— Marks et al. Norms

Three norm sets are presented in both figures. The original MMPI adult norms produce elevations of one standard deviation or more on Scales 4, 6, 7, 8, and 9 for both boys and girls. These scale elevations, although slightly lower on the new MMPI-2 adult norms,[1] persist around one standard deviation above the adult mean on MMPI-2 norms for both boys and girls (Figures 1-1 and 1-2). Preliminary findings similar to these led us to the conclusion that separate adolescent norms would be required for the restandardized MMPI (Williams, Butcher, & Graham, 1986). As seen in Figures 1-1 and 1-2, the Marks et al. (1974) adolescent norms produce scale scores in the 50-60 T-score range. Findings like those illustrated by Figures 1-1 and 1-2 led to the development of separate norms for adolescents (Marks et al., 1974). One of the many areas of controversy in adolescent MMPI interpretation has revolved around the issue of which norm set to use in interpreting an adolescent's profile (i.e., whether one should use the original adult norms or the adolescent norms of Marks et al., 1974).

---

[1] The MMPI-2 adult norms are used here for illustrative purposes only. They should not be used with adolescents.

Code Types

Another area of MMPI differences between adults and adolescents had to do with code types, or the ways in which the clinical scales occurred together. Hathaway and Monachesi's (1963) comparative data, using the adult norm set, showed that adults, particularly women, had more codes suggestive of neurotic problems (i.e., code types characterized by elevations on Scales 1, 2, and 3). Adolescents had sociopathic or psychotic profiles more often than did adults (i.e., code types with elevations on Scales 4, 8, and 9). Subsequent research revealed that the 4-9/9-4 code type, followed by the 2-4/4-2, 3-4/4-3, and 4-6/6-4 code types, occurred most frequently in adolescent clinical samples, regardless of whether the setting was outpatient (Marks et al., 1974) or primarily inpatient (Williams & Butcher, 1989b).

Configural interpretations of individuals' profiles gradually evolved over the years when research with adults indicated that code types provided more useful information than interpretations based on single scale elevations (Graham, 1987, 1990). As mentioned earlier, Marks et al. (1974) used the code-type approach in their large study of adolescents in clinical settings. Unfortunately, the work by these researchers was not replicated for 15 years, and their code-type descriptors remained the only ones based on adolescent responses until the study by Williams and Butcher (1989b). This recent study, using contemporary definitions for code types (e.g., requiring an elevation greater than or equal to an adolescent T score of 65), provided only limited support for the validity of code-type descriptors for adolescents, in contrast to the utility of the code-type approach with adults.

Strategies for MMPI Interpretations for Adolescents

It is generally recognized that MMPI interpretations are less accurate for adolescents than for adults (Archer, 1987; Graham, 1987, 1990; Williams, 1986). In the absence of definitive research about using the MMPI with adolescents, different strategies have evolved for interpreting adolescents' MMPI profiles. As Archer (1987) describes, these strategies are based on assumptions researchers and clinicians make by combining the limited research literature with clinical impressions gained through working with adolescents. Basically, these strategies address which norm set to use with adolescents to convert MMPI raw scores into T scores, as well as which descriptors to use to make interpretations.

MMPI descriptors are determined by elevations on individual scales or on two or more scales (code types). Descriptors frequently are based on correlations between an MMPI scale score and an external criterion measure (e.g., parent, clinician, or teacher ratings or other self-report measures). Thus, descriptors are sometimes referred to as correlates. In this monograph the terms *descriptors* and *correlates* are used interchangeably to refer to empirically established associations between MMPI scales or code types and various criterion measures. Descriptors or correlates are the basis of MMPI interpretive statements.

Established descriptors or correlates can also be a form of validity, most often concurrent or criterion validity. For example, after 50 years of research and use of the MMPI, there are some well-established associations between the MMPI standard scales and external criterion measures (e.g., Scale 1 is related to numerous somatic complaints; Scale 2, to depressive symptoms). When a study replicates these a priori hypothesized relationships, it provides additional evidence of the scales' validity and can be used as a source of scale descriptors. Hathaway and Monachesi's (e.g., 1963) work included evidence of concurrent and criterion validity of the MMPI scales with adolescents, as well as predictive validity (i.e., their prospective study demonstrated that certain MMPI scale elevations in the ninth grade predicted later juvenile delinquency). Similarly, Williams and Butcher (1989a) demonstrated criterion and concurrent validity for the MMPI scales, but only very limited criterion and concurrent validity for MMPI code types during adolescence (Williams & Butcher, 1989b). Both these studies are used as a source of empirically established descriptors for the MMPI standard scales for adolescents.

The Norm Question

Several researchers have compared the effects of using the original adult MMPI norms with using the Marks et al. (1974) adolescent norms on MMPI responses from adolescents. As described earlier, these studies consistently show elevations using the adult norms in general population samples of adolescents (for discussions of the norm issue, see Archer, 1987; Graham, 1990; Williams, 1986). These elevations in general-population adolescent samples typically are not accompanied by other indicators of psychopathology (e.g., Moore & Handel, 1980). Studies of adolescents in clinical settings often reveal pronounced elevations on Scales F (a validity scale; see Table 1-1 for a description), 4, and 8 using the adult norms (e.g., Archer, 1984; Archer, White, & Orvin, 1979; Chase, Chaffin, & Morrison, 1975;

Figure 1-3
Boys Clinical Sample Plotted on Three Different Norms

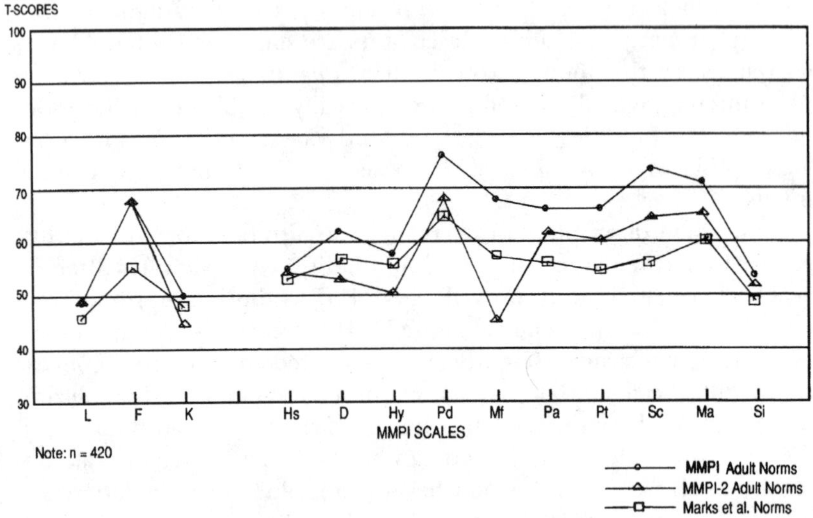

Note: n = 420

———○——— **MMPI** Adult Norms
———△——— MMPI-2 Adult Norms
———□——— Marks et al. Norms

Dudley, Mason, & Hughes, 1972). Demonstration of these elevations has resulted in recommendations that the Marks et al. (1974) adolescent norm set be used exclusively (e.g., Archer, 1984, 1987) or in combination with the adult norm set (e.g., Dahlstrom et al., 1972; Graham, 1987, 1990; Marks et al., 1974; Williams, 1986) in the interpretation of an adolescent's profile. Studies directly examining the clinically rated accuracy of interpretations based on the two norm sets provide some additional support for the use of adolescent norms (e.g., Ehrenworth & Archer, 1985; Klinge, Lachar, Grisell, & Berman, 1978; Lachar, Klinge, & Grisell, 1976).

Those who advocate exclusive use of the adolescent norms are faced with the problem of the large number of false-negative MMPIs (i.e., normal limits profiles) obtained from adolescents in clinical settings, including hospitalized youth. Studies of adolescents in treatment for emotional and behavioral problems most frequently yield mean scores within normal limits on the adolescent norms (e.g., Ehrenworth & Archer, 1985; Klinge, Culbert, & Piggott, 1982; Klinge et al., 1978; Lachar et al., 1976). Similar findings are apparent in the clinical data collected in collaboration with the MMPI Restandardization Project. Figures 1-3 and 1-4 show the effects of the adolescent

Figure 1-4
Girls Clinical Sample Plotted on Three Different Norms

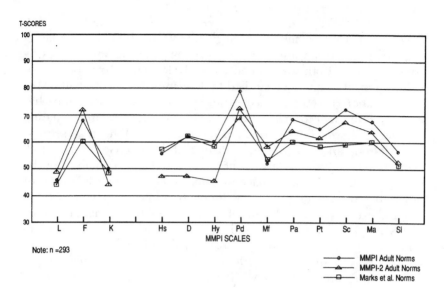

Note: n =293

——○—— MMPI Adult Norms
——△—— MMPI-2 Adult Norms
——□—— Marks et al. Norms

(Marks et al., 1974) and adult norm sets in our large clinical sample of 14- to 18-year-olds. Both the original adult MMPI norms and the new MMPI-2 norms[2] are plotted in Figures 1-3 and 1-4 (see Chapter 2 for further description of this clinical sample). Whereas the original adult norm set yields too many false-positive predictions in general population settings and tends to overpredict psychotic disturbances in clinical settings, the Marks et al. (1974) norm set yields too many false-negative predictions in clinical settings, as Figures 1-3 and 1-4 indicate. It is important to mention here that we have other assessment information on these subjects that indicates the presence of significant psychopathology (e.g., Williams, Ben-Porath, Uchiyama, Weed, & Archer, 1990; Williams, Ben-Porath, & Weed, 1990). This catch-22 of adolescent MMPI interpretations is what led us to recommend that profiles from both norm sets be plotted and interpretations drawn from each, although we also suggest giving somewhat more weight to the adolescent norm set (see Graham, 1990; Williams, 1986). Another way to correct the false-negative problem in clinical settings is to use an ado-

---

[2] Again, the MMPI-2 adult norms are used here for illustrative purposes only. They should not be used with adolescents.

lescent T-score cutoff of 65, rather than the traditional T score of 70 used with adults, to define clinical significance (Archer, 1987; Ehrenworth & Archer, 1985).

Two potential replacements have been proposed for the Marks et al. (1974) adolescent norms (i.e., Colligan & Offord, 1989; Gottesman et al., 1987). Both of these norm sets are included as appendices by Archer (1987). Both are limited clinically for several reasons. First, neither norm set has been studied to determine the validity of MMPI interpretations based on its scores, and one study suggests that each is roughly equivalent to the Marks et al. (1974) norms in discriminating among adolescents in outpatient, inpatient, and normal settings (Klinefelter, Pancoast, Archer, & Pruitt, 1990). The Gottesman et al. (1987) norms, although labeled new, are based on a reanalysis of the original Hathaway and Monachesi data set. Given the publication of norms based on a contemporary sample of adolescents by the MMPI Restandardization Project, clinical use of a reanalysis of data from the 1940s and 1950s would seem only to further confuse, rather than illuminate, the interpretation of adolescents' profiles.

The Colligan and Offord (1989) norms have limited clinical application for several reasons. MMPIs were collected from subjects in three midwestern states (Minnesota, Iowa, and Wisconsin) who completed instruments mailed to their homes. Thus, the data were not derived from a representative sample of young people in the United States, and the mail-out procedure did not ensure the required supervised administration. Another limitation was the use of a T-score generation procedure that resulted in T scores that were not comparable to traditional MMPI T scores. Rather than using linear T scores, as Hathaway and McKinley (1940) did with the original MMPI norms for adults and Marks et al. (1974) did with the adolescent norms, Colligan and Offord used a normalized T-score approach, which, as depicted in the MMPI-2 manual (Butcher, Dahlstrom, Graham, Tellegen, & Kaemmer, 1989), results in considerable attenuation of T scores at clinically meaningful levels of scale elevation (see Chapter 4 for further discussion).

A possible advantage of using the Colligan and Offord (1989) norm set for adolescent interpretations would be to provide for Pancoast and Archer's (1988) conclusion that "meaningful changes have occurred in the response patterns of adolescents since the creation of the Marks et al. (1974) norms" (p. 699). However, these changes more likely are due to instructional differences in MMPI administration over the years. When the Marks et al. (1974) norms were collected, Cannot Say (see Table 1-1) responding was not discouraged, as it is in contemporary practice. Hathaway and Monachesi (1963) allowed their subjects to omit items they did not understand or felt did not apply to them. However, in more recent data collection, and in actual use of the MMPI in clinical settings, individuals are encouraged to respond to all the items. Consequently, when comparing normative data across time, one needs to recognize that item omissions in the early studies result in lower raw scores than are obtained in more contemporary studies.

In addition to deciding which norm set to use, clinicians are faced with decisions about which descriptors to use to make interpretations. Should one use adult-derived code-type descriptors as presented in Graham (1987), or should one use the adolescent-derived code-type descriptors as introduced by Marks et al. (1974)? What about using the combined adult/adolescent code-type approach as recommended by Archer (1987)? More recently, a scale-descriptor approach has been suggested by the data in Williams and Butcher (1989a, 1989b). A brief description of several of the more common adolescent interpretive strategies follows.

Adult Interpretive Approach

This interpretive strategy relies on the original adult MMPI norms and the adult code-type descriptors (i.e., the standard approach for making MMPI interpretations for adults). Use of the adult interpretive approach can be traced to Hathaway and Monachesi (1963) with their explicit statement, "We do not advocate the use of special juvenile norms with the MMPI, since to do so would arbitrarily erase much of the contrast between adolescents and adults" (p. 39). However, Hathaway and Monachesi recognized the need for clinicians to take into account the basic differences in adolescents' responses to the MMPI with their suggestion that the mean profile of normal adolescents, along with a line representing two standard deviations above this mean, be plotted on any given adolescent's profile sheet. Presumably, this practice would allow clinicians to consider normative differences among adults and adolescents when making interpretations, although Hathaway and Monachesi did not elaborate on how this might be done.

Other users of the adult interpretive strategy developed a procedure that has been called the "eyeball approach" (Williams, 1986). In this approach, the adult norms and adult code-type descriptors are used, but clinicians mentally adjust the adolescent's profile, taking into consideration the normative differences (e.g., an extreme elevation on Scale 4 would be "reduced" when it appeared on an adolescent's profile). No clear decision rules have ever been presented for this approach. Williams (1986) presents case examples illustrating the unacceptability of the eyeball method. However, it continues to have its users.

Adolescent Interpretive Approach

Along with developing adolescent norms for the MMPI, Marks et al. (1974) also presented adolescent-derived code-type descriptors, allowing for interpretations using both age-appropriate norms and code-type descriptors. In their actuarial study of two-point code types, Marks et al. incorporated 29 two-point code types along with a profile type depicting an average adolescent patient. To obtain behavioral descriptors for their MMPI code types, they used several rating forms with a preliminary pool of 2,302 descriptions based on self-report and therapist ratings. They narrowed the final pool of personality and symptom descriptors down to 1,265 for their study. In deriving code-type descriptors for their actuarial system, Marks et al. employed a relatively small minimum number of cases (10) for each code studied. Marks et al. did not advocate the exclusive use of their adolescent interpretive approach. Rather, like Dahlstrom et al. (1972), they suggested combining the use of an adult interpretive approach with their newly developed adolescent interpretive strategy.

Mixed Interpretive Approach

In this strategy, the adolescent norms (Marks et al., 1974) were used in combination with the adult code-type descriptors available in interpretive manuals such as Graham's (1987). It evolved because of problems with the accuracy of interpretations based on the adult and adolescent approaches. These three primary approaches were studied for accuracy.

Ehrenworth and Archer (1985) examined the accuracy, as rated by adolescents' clinicians, of the three primary interpretive approaches: (a) the adult interpretive strategy (adult norms/adult code-type descriptors), (b) the adolescent interpretive strategy (adolescent norms/ adolescent descriptors), and (c) the mixed approach (adolescent norms/adult descriptors). The source for both the adult and adolescent descriptors was Marks et al. (1974). Ehrenworth and Archer's overall conclusion supports the generally accepted notion that MMPI interpretations for adolescents are less accurate than those for adults. Of the three interpretive strategies examined, the adult and mixed approaches were rated more accurate than the adolescent approach. However, the small sample size in this study, along with the exclusive reliance on descriptors from Marks et al. (1974) rather than more contemporary sources (e.g., Graham, 1977; Greene, 1980), are limitations to consider.

Combined Interpretive Approach

Archer (1987) developed two-point code-type descriptors for the 29 code types presented in Marks et al. (1974), using what could be called a combined approach. He combined the adolescent descriptors found in Marks et al. (1974) with the adult descriptors available in Graham (1977), Greene (1980), and Lachar (1974), providing narrative descriptions for each of the 29 code types. These narratives typically began with statements found to be common in the adolescent and adult sources and concluded with information found only in one, but not the others. Archer (1987) suggests that the descriptors found in both adolescent and adult sources might be considered more "robust," although he also indicates that "this assumption is speculative and represents this author's 'best guess' given the research literature and clinical experience surrounding the interpretation of adolescent profiles" (pp. 65-66).

Scale Descriptor Interpretive Approach

This approach is based on findings demonstrating that many traditional MMPI scale descriptors found in adult studies replicated in a large adolescent clinical sample (Williams & Butcher, 1989a). On the other hand, Williams and Butcher (1989b) found only limited support for the traditional adult code-type descriptors (e.g., Graham, 1987), the adolescent code-type descriptors (Marks et al., 1974), or the combined code-type descriptors (Archer, 1987) when using the suggested adolescent T-score cutoff of 65 to define a code type. As the name implies, this approach uses scale descriptors, rather than code-type descriptors, as the primary information source for making interpretations. Furthermore, raw score cutoffs, not T scores, were provided because of the problems with the adolescent norms (Williams & Butcher, 1989a).

A Closer Examination of the MMPI and Adolescents

Our review reveals support for the concurrent and predictive validity of the MMPI with adolescents (e.g., Archer et al., 1988; Ehrenworth &

Archer, 1985; Hathaway & Monachesi, 1963; Hathaway et al., 1969; Lipovsky, Finch, & Belter, 1989; Williams & Butcher, 1989a, 1989b; Wirt & Briggs, 1959). However, as the number of interpretive strategies described above indicates, adolescent MMPI interpretation is complex and controversial. No interpretive strategy for adolescents emerges with the level of accuracy demonstrated in studies of adults. The various methods described above attempt to increase the accuracy of MMPI interpretations for adolescents. Developing an adolescent norm set and code-type descriptors (Marks et al., 1974), changing the adolescent T-score cutoff from 70 to 65 (Archer, 1987; Ehrenworth & Archer, 1985), combining descriptors from adults and adolescents (Archer, 1987), and other effects are laudable attempts to improve the accuracy of MMPI interpretations for adolescents. Yet, on closer examination, each approach seems to introduce other problems or issues.

Most of the previous attempts to improve the MMPI's validity with adolescents focused on refinements at the norm- and scale-descriptor levels, to the neglect of item content or scale development. Sporadic efforts to develop scales for adolescents have occurred throughout the MMPI's history, but no attempts were made to improve the item content for adolescents until the MMPI Restandardization Project began.

Item-Level Issues

Many of the item-level problems on the MMPI were troublesome to both adults and adolescents. Out-of-date phrases, awkward wording, objectionable content, and other stylistic problems contributed to the confusion and annoyance of test takers. The original items did not adequately assess some important areas: suicide, marijuana and other drug use, motivation for treatment, and change potential. Items assessing these problems were added to the MMPI by the Restandardization Committee for both adults and adolescents.

A number of item-level problems unique to adolescents also remained, hence the Restandardization Committee's decision to develop an experimental booklet to use in studies of adolescents (Form TX; see Chapter 2 for a description). Since the original MMPI item pool had relatively few themes specific to adolescents and their problems, more items assessing areas such as peer group influence, family relations, school, and teachers were added to the experimental adolescent booklet. The ability of these new items to enhance the MMPI's validity with adolescents would determine whether a separate form of the MMPI should be developed for adolescents. Because this decision was not made at the onset of the Restandardization Project, but depended on data collected during the project, all the original MMPI items, edited to improve grammar and style, were included in Form TX. This meant that some of the original MMPI items considered inappropriate for younger adolescents (e.g., "My sex life is satisfactory") were included in TX. Other items about behaviors occurring during the adolescent period were worded in the past tense on the original MMPI (e.g., "Sometimes when I was young I stole things") and were included without change on TX as well, although these verb tense problems were corrected in the newly developed MMPI-A.

One final item-level issue for adolescents has to do with the number of items on the MMPI. Many clinicians point out that a 566-item booklet is simply too long for most young people in clinical settings. Some adolescents referred for psychological assessment do not have the necessary attention and concentration skills to complete such a long booklet. Clearly, trade-offs have to be made between amount of material assessed and the need for a shorter test. With the MMPI Restandardization Project, the University of Minnesota Press decided to study these item-level issues. However, the lack of work at the item level does not account for the lack of MMPI scale development for adolescents over the years.

Scale Development and Adolescents

Hathaway and Monachesi (1957, 1963) provided an example of scale development work with adolescents, albeit an unsuccessful one. They reported an attempt to develop a scale for selecting those predelinquent boys who would later appear in police or court records. They used the Minneapolis sample of 1,958 boys followed at two and four years after the original MMPI testing in ninth grade. The boys' delinquency ratings ranged from very minor offenses found in police records (e.g., parking violations) to repeated serious offenses (e.g., auto theft, burglary, armed robbery). The researchers initially identified 33 items that cross-validated in comparisons of delinquents and nondelinquents (Hathaway & Monachesi, 1957), and eventually refined the Delinquency Scale (De) to 30 items (Hathaway & Monachesi, 1963).

Hathaway and Monachesi (1963) were disappointed with the predictive validity of the De Scale. They concluded that they were unable to develop a scale to measure delinquency proneness in young boys accurately using MMPI items. They believed the problem was with the diversity of the personalities of boys who later become delinquent: "For example, it does not appear likely that a boy who steals to help get food for his family would have the same score on a scale of delinquency proneness as would a boy who steals because he wants to buy a motorcycle for racing" (p. 90). In addition, using only a personality measure to predict delinquency proneness ignored many other factors likely related to this problem.

Another issue to consider in evaluating the limited predictive validity of the De Scale has to do with the adequacy of the criterion measures used by Hathaway and Monachesi (i.e., police and court records). More recent definitions of delinquent behavior are not limited to those acts coming to the attention of authorities (Gold & Petronio, 1980). The use of official records to identify delinquents probably results in a misclassification of adolescents engaging in delinquent behaviors as nondelinquents. It seems likely that a personality measure would be most strongly related to whether the adolescent exhibits the behaviors, not to whether he or she is caught by the authorities.

Substance abuse is another area where some scale-level studies have been carried out with adolescents. The validity of the MacAndrew Alcoholism Scale (MAC), originally empirically developed to differentiate alcoholic from nonalcoholic adult psychiatric patients (MacAndrew, 1965), has been investigated frequently with adolescent substance abusers (e.g., Klinge et al., 1978; Moore, 1984, 1985; Wisniewski, Glenwick, & Graham, 1985; Wolfson & Erbaugh, 1984). MacAndrew (1986) empirically developed a new 36-item MMPI-derived scale, the Substance Abuse Proclivity (SAP) Scale, to detect proneness to substance abuse in younger boys and men (ages 16-22). He concluded that the SAP Scale was a more "youth-oriented phrasing of the general reward-seeking orientation" characterizing high scorers on the MAC (p. 166).

A more recent example of the necessity of further scale refinement for adolescents is the MMPI Restandardization Project's work on the F Scale. The F Scale consistently appears as one of the most elevated scales in adolescent clinical samples. Archer (1987) reports that using the conservative adult standard to define profile invalidity (i.e., F ≥ 16) seems unwarranted, given the large number of cases that would be defined as invalid (i.e., between 34% and 44% in clinical settings) and the meaningful descriptors associated with high F responding (e.g., acting-out behaviors, psychotic symptoms). Gallucci (1987) suggests that the F Scale does not measure motivation to exaggerate symptoms or a "plea for help"; rather, elevated F scores are a feature of the modal adolescent MMPI profile. Given its straightforward method of development (see Table 1-1), it is interesting that no earlier attempts were made to refine the F Scale for adolescents. The MMPI Restandardization Project examined the endorsement percentages of F Scale items for the adolescent normative sample and identified 17 new infrequent items for an adolescent version of F. Other original F items were deleted because of objectionable content, for space reasons when a particular item appeared only on F, or because the item was not infrequent in an adolescent sample (Butcher et al., 1992).

Future Directions: Content Scales for Adolescents

This chapter has provided a synopsis of many issues and controversies surrounding the use of the MMPI standard scales with adolescents. Although the MMPI has been one of the most frequently used psychological tests with adolescents, MMPI interpretations are less accurate for adolescents than for adults. Over the 50 years since the MMPI's development, several attempts have been made to improve the instrument's validity with adolescents, mostly focusing on norms and code-type descriptors. Until the MMPI Restandardization Project was undertaken, there were no efforts at item-level improvements and very few scale-level refinements.

Little past research focuses on the development or use of content scales for adolescents. Content scales are based upon assumptions that are different from those of the empirically derived standard scales. The primary interpretive strategy for the standard or empirical scales involves simply listing the established correlates or descriptors of the scales. Content-based measures, on the other hand, can be interpreted by reference to the dimensions being assessed by the items making up the scale. This process has been shown to be as valid as empirical interpretation strategies (e.g., Burisch, 1984; Butcher, Graham, Williams, & Ben-Porath, 1990; Holden & Fekken, 1990). Content scale interpretation for adolescents has been suggested to enhance the MMPI's validity in this age group. However, content scale interpretation for adolescents has been hampered by lack of research, including normative data from the general population. One of the few existing studies on content scales and adolescents presents raw score means and standard deviations in an adolescent psychiatric sample, but not information from a true normative sample (Watson, Harris, Johnson, & LaBeck, 1983). Our effort to develop content scales for adolescents is the first major attempt to refine the MMPI for adolescents that addresses issues and problems at the item, scale, norm, and descriptor levels. The remainder of this monograph details our work in developing content scales for the new MMPI-A.

Chapter 2

Methods Used in Developing the MMPI-A

The research program described in this book parallels the development of the MMPI-A for adolescents detailed in the MMPI-A manual (Butcher et al., 1992). Many of the instruments, procedures, and normative and clinical samples used in the development of the MMPI-A were also used in the development of the MMPI-A Content Scales. This chapter summarizes the methods followed in the larger project, providing the context for our work on the MMPI-A Content Scales. The MMPI Restandardization Project, sponsored by the University of Minnesota Press, represents the first revision and restandardization of the instrument in its 50-year history.

At the beginning of the MMPI Restandardization Project in 1982, the committee decided to investigate whether alterations in the items and booklet would make the MMPI a more viable instrument for adolescents. At this early stage, no explicit decision was made to develop a separate adolescent form of the instrument. No radical deviations from the past were implemented for adolescents at the beginning of the project. An experimental version of the inventory, Form TX, was developed and used in the data collection for adolescents. Form AX, the adult experimental version used to develop the MMPI-2, was not used in the adolescent studies. The decision about whether to develop an adolescent version of the MMPI was deferred until data collected during the project demonstrated a need for and utility of a special form for adolescents.

Development of Form TX and the Subsequent MMPI-A

In many respects the development of Form TX paralleled the work on the experimental booklet (Form AX) for adults. Both Forms TX and AX contained the 550 items from the original MMPI with slight wording alterations. The 16 repeated items in the original MMPI were deleted from Forms AX and TX, allowing for the addition of some new items. Items with awkward or archaic language were rewritten (see Ben-Porath & Butcher, 1989; Butcher et al., 1989, for a discussion of the changes in the original MMPI items). New items were added to both Forms AX and TX addressing treatment compliance, attitudes toward self-change, amenability to therapy, relationship problems, and problems with alcohol and other drugs. Also included in Form TX were more than 50 new items with adolescent-specific content. These were written by James Butcher, John Graham, and Carolyn Williams after reviewing research on adolescent problem behavior and considering clinical issues in work with adolescents. The new items were developed to assess youthful behavior problems and attitudes, such as peer group influences, school behavior, attitudes toward teachers, eating problems, and relationships with family and other adults. By the time the MMPI-2 manual was published (Butcher et al., 1989), initial analyses of the normative data (Williams et al., 1986) and clinical studies of the MMPI standard scales (Williams & Butcher, 1989a) and code types (Williams & Butcher, 1989b) suggested that, at the least, new adolescent norms were needed, and serious consideration should be given to the development of a separate booklet for adolescents.

After the publication of MMPI-2, the original MMPI Restandardization Committee (James Butcher, Grant Dahlstrom, John Graham, and Auke Tellegen) was reconstituted in 1989 by Beverly Kaemmer of the University of Minnesota Press, and full attention turned to the adolescent data and the question of whether a specific adolescent form of the MMPI was needed. The new committee members appointed to complete the adolescent version of the MMPI were James Butcher, Auke Tellegen, and Robert Archer. John Graham, Carolyn Williams, and Yossef Ben-Porath continued their efforts as collaborators in MMPI research. By the beginning of 1990, the University of Minnesota Press became committed to the publication of an adolescent version of the instrument, the MMPI-A.

In 1990 the Adolescent MMPI Project Committee, after an extensive period of evaluation and consultation, reduced the 704-item TX booklet to the 478-item MMPI-A (Butcher et al., 1992). One primary goal was to reduce the item pool of Form TX so that adolescents would be more willing and motivated to complete the test in a shorter testing session than required for the MMPI-2. Williams, Ben-Porath, and Hevern (1991) presented information from a subsample of the normative subjects indicating that this was highly desirable and should increase the acceptability of the instrument with young people. The desire to shorten the booklet was balanced with the need to ensure that it would retain measures found to be effective in assessing adolescent problems and behaviors. (Content validity of MMPI-A will be covered in Chapter 3.)

The first stage in reducing Form TX item content was to ensure that the original validity and standard scales of the MMPI were maintained relatively intact in the MMPI-A. In addition, items making up the new content scales for adolescents were included. Finally, several other supplementary scales from the original MMPI were maintained in the MMPI-A because they showed some promise for adolescent assessment (i.e., MAC, A, and R), as was the newly developed MMPI-A Immaturity supplementary scale. Two rather lengthy standard scales from the original MMPI, Scales 5 and 0, were shortened slightly. Once the scale composition for the MMPI-A was determined, any remaining items not scored on these scales were deleted from the booklet. Special emphasis also was placed upon deletion of items judged to be objectionable in the assessment of adolescent behavior (e.g., the item assuming sexual activity was eliminated).

During our initial development of the MMPI-A Content Scales, we found 19 items from the original MMPI referring to youthful problems in the past tense (e.g., "I liked school"; "My parents often objected to the kind of people I went around with"). This occurred because of the initial decision to keep the original MMPI item content the same in Forms TX and AX. However, when the decision to develop a separate adolescent booklet was made, these 19 items were judged to be inappropriately worded. Therefore, Williams, Ben-Porath, and Hevern (1991) studied the effect of rewriting these items in the present tense for the MMPI-A. Results indicated that the rewritten items did not hamper the psychometric performance of the MMPI-A's validity, standard, or content scales. Therefore, the rewritten versions of these 19 items were included in the MMPI-A booklet. A second study to evaluate the effects of rewriting items was conducted in a one-week test-retest research design. The 19 rewritten items from the first study were included, with 7 additional items that were rewritten to clarify ambiguity. The older (MMPI) version of the items was given on one occasion and the revised version on another in counterbalanced order. The results of this study, reported in the MMPI-A manual (Butcher et al., 1992), were that test-retest stability of rewritten items was comparable to test-retest of items that were not changed.

Measures Used with Normative and Clinical Samples

In addition to Form TX, adolescent subjects were administered several other measures, depending upon their sample or site. Three mea-

TABLE 2-1. Number of subjects by measures for the normative and clinical samples

Setting	Form TX	BIO	LE	RR	DAB	CBCL	TRF	YSR	DICA	DISC
						Measures				
Normative sample										
805 boys	805 (100)	805 (100)	805 (100)	0	0	75 (9)	47 (6)	84 (10)	0	57 (7)
815 girls	815 (100)	815 (100)	815 (100)	0	0	82 (10)	52 (6)	95 (12)	0	63 (8)
Clinical sample (total)										
420 boys	420 (100)	411 (98)	409 (97)	412 (98)	313 (75)	279 (66)	37 (9)	0	271 (66)	0
293 girls	243 (100)	278 (95)	277 (95)	284 (97)	221 (75)	202 (69)	6 (2)	0	188 (77)	0
Alcohol/drug units										
299 boys	299 (100)	297 (99)	295 (99)	296 (99)	245 (82)	220 (74)	0	0	181 (61)	0
163 girls	163 (100)	160 (98)	158 (97)	160 (98)	123 (75)	126 (77)	0	0	93 (57)	0
Psychiatric units										
67 boys	67 (100)	65 (97)	65 (97)	67 (100)	57 (85)	59 (88)	0	0	47 (70)	0
96 girls	96 (100)	91 (95)	92 (96)	94 (98)	75 (78)	76 (79)	0	0	66 (69)	0
Special schools										
41 boys	41 (100)	40 (98)	40 (98)	38 (93)	0	0	37 (90)	0	35 (85)	0
10 girls	10 (100)	9 (90)	9 (90)	8 (80)	0	0	6 (60)	0	5 (50)	0
Day treatment										
13 boys	13 (100)	9 (69)	9 (69)	11 (85)	11 (85)	0	0	0	8 (62)	0
24 girls	24 (100)	18 (75)	18 (75)	22 (92)	23 (96)	0	0	0	13 (54)	0

Note: Numbers in parentheses are percentages of the indicated samples completing the different instruments. Form TX is the experimental adolescent version of the MMPI, BIO refers to Biographical Information Form, LE to Life Events Form, RR to Record Review, DAB to Devereux Adolescent Behavior Rating Scale, CBCL to Child Behavior Checklist, TRF to Teacher Report Form, YSR to Youth Self-Report Form, DICA to Diagnostic Interview for Children and Adolescents, and DISC to the Diagnostic Interview Schedule for Children.

sures, Form TX and two other instruments developed for the Restandardization Project (i.e., the Biographical Information Form and the Life Events Form; see Appendixes A and B in this volume), formed the core battery administered to all subjects regardless of sample or site. A battery of standardized clinical measures was added to the data collection in the clinical samples to provide additional criterion variables for scale correlate studies. These criterion measures were used in our studies of the MMPI standard scales and code types (Williams & Butcher, 1989a, 1989b). One small subsample of the normative subjects was also administered several of these additional criterion measures, although time and funding constraints did not allow continued collection of these measures at the normative sites. All the measures used in the adolescent data collection are described below, beginning with the two from the core battery. Table 2-1 indicates the number of subjects in each of the settings completing the various instruments described below. The clinical sites were all community-based facilities located in the Minneapolis area.

Biographical Information Form

This brief form, developed for the Restandardization Project, asked for demographic information, including age, religion, ethnic origin, grade level, average school grades, school activities, school problems, future plans, father's and mother's educational levels, father's and mother's occupations, number of siblings, and current living arrangements. The Biographical Information Form was completed by the subjects and is reproduced in Appendix A.

Life Events Form

This form was modified from the work of Coddington (1972) for the MMPI Restandardization Project. Subjects were requested to indicate if any of a list of 74 life events had happened to them in the last six months. If an event had occurred, they then were asked if it had a positive, negative, or no effect on them. The Life Events Form is included here as Appendix B.

Record Review Form

A standardized form to facilitate a thorough review of each subject's hospital chart or school records was developed for the clinical sites (see

Appendix C). The charts or records were reviewed by nine trained research assistants who met weekly to ensure consistency across raters. The raters were asked not to review MMPI profiles prior to completing the Record Review Form. A total of 34 record review variables, with information about presenting problems and behaviors, suicide, sexual and physical abuse, court or social service involvement, and so forth, were selected as potential MMPI descriptors. Seven of these clinical entities, such as bizarre behaviors, occurred in less than 10% of the sample. However, because of their salience as MMPI descriptors, these low-frequency variables were included in the analyses.

The interrater reliability for the Record Review Form was evaluated by having raters complete ratings independently for the same subject in a total of 177 cases (14% of subjects for whom Record Review Forms were obtained). Kappas were computed using Fleiss's (1971) formula for nominal scale agreement with many raters. All but one (i.e., poor social skills) of the remaining 27 variables of interest had agreement exceeding the .05 level of significance. Although they were significant, the magnitudes of some of the significant kappas were often low (e.g., .25). We did not drop any of these items from the analyses because of limited reliability, but it is important to note that low reliability occurred with some of the empirical descriptors in the Record Review Form. This, coupled with infrequency of the behaviors in the sample, would tend to lower validity coefficients, providing conservative validity estimates (Williams & Butcher, 1989a, 1989b).

Devereux Adolescent Behavior Rating Scale

The Devereux Adolescent Behavior Rating Scale (DAB), developed by Spivack and colleagues (Spivack, Haimes, & Spotts, 1967; Spivack & Spotts, 1967), provided behavior ratings from treatment staff focusing upon a broad range of clinical symptoms and behaviors. The counselors and nursing staff in several of our clinical sites completed the DAB. They were instructed to complete the rating prior to looking at the MMPI profiles. Raters were closely guided by research assistants to assure that the treatment staff followed standard procedures, understood the importance of independent DAB ratings, and made their observations without reference to other psychometric data.

The 84 items of the DAB covered a broad range of problem behaviors of disturbed adolescents in easily understood language, requiring little inference on the part of the rater. The original DAB scales were not developed from the instrument's present item list (Spivack et al., 1967; Spivack & Spotts, 1967). Moreover, our previous research with the DAB (Ben-Porath, Williams, & Uchiyama, 1989; Williams,

Ben-Porath, Uchiyama, Weed, & Archer, 1990; Williams, Ben-Porath, & Weed, 1990) revealed low internal consistencies and high interscale correlations in those original scales in samples that included subjects from the present clinical sample. Because of this, we used the new scales we developed for the DAB (Ben-Porath et al., 1989) as criterion measures for our content scales. These DAB scales were developed using item-level factor analysis and proved to be reliable and valid measures of Acting Out Behaviors (AOB Scale), Withdrawn/Timid Behaviors (WTB Scale), Psychotic Behaviors (PB Scale), Neurotic/Dependent Behaviors (NDB Scale), and Heterosexual Interests (HI Scale) (Williams, Ben-Porath, Uchiyama, Weed, & Archer, 1990). Although the data used in the construction of these new scales came from many of the same subjects used in the present research, the development of factorially based scales for the DAB precludes any confounding between the construction of these scales and their use as extratest criterion measures in the evaluation of the MMPI-A Content Scales.

Child Behavior Checklist

The Child Behavior Checklist (CBCL) was developed by Achenbach and Edelbrock (1983) for children ages 6 to 16. We obtained the authors' permission to make slight wording changes (e.g., the word *child* was changed to *teenager*) to develop a form more appropriate for older adolescents (Achenbach, personal communication, January 1985). The computer scoring program provided by Achenbach was used for scoring, and raw scores were used in the analyses because normative scores were not available for our older subjects. Parents did not have information from their children's evaluations before making their ratings. Both the behavior problems and social competence scales for boys and girls on the CBCL were used as potential MMPI descriptors. The social competence scales were the same for both genders and included parents' reports of their adolescents' participation and performance in areas designated as Activities, Social, and School. The behavior problem scales for boys included Aggressive, Delinquent, Hostile Withdrawal, Hyperactive, Immature, Obsessive-Compulsive, Schizoid, Somatic Complaints, Uncommunicative, Internalizing, Externalizing, and Total. The behavior problem scales for girls included Aggressive, Anxious-Obsessive, Cruel, Delinquent, Depressed Withdrawal, Immature-Hyperactive, Schizoid, Somatic Complaints, Internalizing, Externalizing, and Total. Although some of the CBCL scales had the same names for boys and girls, their item content could differ.

A majority of the subjects in our clinical settings and a small subsample of the normative subjects were rated on the CBCL. Only CBCL data from the clinical settings were used in the validity analyses in this monograph. The CBCL scores from the normative subsample were used in another study to identify potentially deviant subjects (Williams, Hearn, Hostetler, & Ben-Porath, 1991).

Teacher Report Form

The Teacher Report Form (TRF), designed to be completed by teachers who had known a student for at least two months, was modeled on the CBCL (Achenbach & Edelbrock, 1986). As with the CBCL, we obtained the authors' permission for slight wording changes to improve the instrument's face validity for older adolescents (Achenbach, personal communication, January 1985). The computer scoring program provided by Achenbach was used. Teachers were blind to an individual's MMPI scores when completing the TRF. The TRF was used with very small subsamples from both normative and clinical settings, but the number of completed instruments was too small to provide adequate power for our correlate analyses of the content scales. TRF data collected from a subsample of the normative sample were used in another study to identify potentially deviant subjects (Williams, Hearn, Hostetler, & Ben-Porath, 1991). TRF data collected in the special school setting from the clinical sample were used in the review of subjects selected for inclusion in the case descriptions for Chapter 6. The TRFs were not used in any of the analyses presented in this monograph.

Youth Self-Report Form

The Youth Self-Report Form (YSR), a self-report behavior checklist for adolescents (11 to 18 years), parallels the CBCL and TRF (Achenbach & Edelbrock, 1987). Many of the same behaviors covered in the CBCL and TRF were included on the YSR. Achenbach's computer scoring program was used to obtain profiles of age-appropriate T scores. The YSR was used with a small subsample of the normative subjects described by Williams, Hearn, Hostetler, and Ben-Porath (1991). As with the TRF, the YSR scores were not used in the validity analyses described in this monograph.

Diagnostic Interview for Children and Adolescents

When clinical data collection began in 1985, Steven Stein of Multi-Health Systems of Toronto, the distributor of the computerized version of the Diagnostic Interview for Children and Adolescents (DICA), began a collaborative project with Williams and Butcher by providing the DICA and technical assistance. This version of the DICA provided *DSM-III* diagnoses in the following areas: attention deficit disorder, oppositional disorders, conduct disorders, substance abuse, affective disorders, anxiety disorders, eating disorders, somatization, enuresis/encopresis, gender identity/sexual expression, and psychosis. In addition, the DICA presented questions about demographic background and psychosocial stressors. Not all the items in the interview were administered; there was branching of items depending upon the adolescent's responses. Herjanic and her colleagues did early developmental work with the DICA (e.g., Herjanic & Campbell, 1977; Herjanic, Herjanic, Brown, & Wheatt, 1975; Herjanic & Reich, 1982). The DICA was selected for use with our clinical subjects because of the earlier work on its reliability and validity, and because it was available as a computer-administered instrument. The DICA took approximately one and one-half to two hours to administer by computer, and was completed by 459 clinical subjects. A separate study presented a comparison of the DICA and MMPI-A (Ben-Porath & Williams, 1991). DICA diagnoses and responses were used in writing the case descriptions presented in Chapter 6.

Diagnostic Interview Schedule for Children

The Diagnostic Interview Schedule for Children (DISC) was developed by the National Institute of Mental Health to extend the use of the Diagnostic Interview Schedule (DIS) to epidemiological studies of children and adolescents from 6 to 17 years (Gutterman, O'Brien, & Young, 1987). It is a structured diagnostic interview, designed to be administered by lay interviewers, and yields *DSM-III* diagnoses at two severity levels (i.e., possible or probable). Version XV.II (Costello, Edelbrock, Kalas, Kessler, & Klaric, 1983) was administered by an experienced clinician (Williams) to a small subsample of the normative subjects during 1985. The computer scoring program was provided by A. J. Costello. Williams, Hearn, Hostetler, and Ben-Porath (1991) describe a comparison of the DISC, YSR, and original MMPI. The DISC was not used in any analyses presented in this monograph.

Procedures Used for Normative Data Collection

The subjects recruited for the development of the MMPI-A norms were obtained from several junior and senior high schools in various geographic regions of the United States. These locations were selected to obtain a generally representative sample of adolescents from diverse regions, rural and urban residences, and different ethnic backgrounds. Local psychologists were recruited from each site to serve as project coordinators.

Informed Consent

Permission to collect data was obtained from school administrators in the various districts. An active parental consent procedure was used in all normative data collection sites, with the exception of our last site, a New York City high school, where a passive consent procedure was used. The active consent procedure required that a parent return an informed consent form before his or her son or daughter was eligible for participation. Students were eligible for participation in the passive consent procedure if parents did *not* return forms or telephone the school. The adolescents' cooperation was maintained during the testing sessions, although subjects were free to leave the study at any time.

Test Administration Procedures

In cooperation with the school principal or assistant principal, the project coordinator at each data-collection site established the most appropriate and efficient testing procedures from the school's perspective. The various schools differed in their procedures for research, requiring flexibility in how the testing session was organized. The number of sessions, when they were scheduled, whether the testing was done during or after school, transportation to and from school, and so forth, were arranged separately for each participating school. However, most of the testing was scheduled in afternoon or early evening, after regular school hours, in vacant classrooms or auditoriums. Students were tested in groups ranging from 5 to 100 subjects. The number of proctors varied at each site, but usually there was approximately one proctor per 25 subjects, depending upon the number of students being tested.

The test battery was group administered in approximately three-hour sessions that included periodic breaks. In some instances, the tests were administered in two separate sessions, a day or so apart. In most cases, students were paid $10.00 for their participation when they turned in completed materials. A subgroup of students from three sites participated in the test-retest study, taking the test battery twice, one week apart. Students participating in the test-retest study were paid an additional $10.00 for the second administration. In most schools the subjects' participation was anonymous. In all schools their data were kept confidential.

Description of the Adolescent Normative Sample

Criteria for Excluding Cases

In order to assure that only complete and valid protocols from cooperative subjects were included in the normative sample, several criteria were used to exclude cases. Only subjects who completed all three Restandardization Project forms (i.e., Form TX, the Biographical Information Form, and the Life Events Form) were included in the normative sample. In addition, records with a Cannot Say raw score on Form TX greater than or equal to 35 and an original F raw score greater than or equal to 25 were eliminated.

Demographic Characteristics of the Normative Sample

We did not have demographic information from parental report or from objective, external data sources. The demographic information included here was obtained from the adolescents' self-report. Such reports of variables such as parental occupation, parental education, and so forth may be inexact to an unknown degree. The reader should keep this in mind when reviewing this section. Demographic information was obtained from the Biographical Information Form, which was completed at the same time that Form TX was administered.

Region. Table 2-2 presents the numbers and percentages of subjects in the normative sample from various testing sites in Minnesota, New York, North Carolina, Ohio, California, Virginia, Pennsylvania, and Washington. Geographic representation was attained with normative

TABLE 2-2. Regions of subjects in the normative sample

Region	Boys (n = 805)		Girls (n = 815)	
	Frequency	%	Frequency	%
Minnesota	201	25.0	300	36.8
New York	168	20.9	0	0.0
North Carolina	119	14.8	84	10.3
Ohio	101	12.5	109	13.4
California	99	12.3	127	15.6
Virginia	82	10.2	127	15.6
Pennsylvania	34	4.2	55	6.7
Washington State*	1	0.1	13	1.6

*The American Indian Reservation (Muckleshoot) sample contains all of the subjects between 14 and 18 years old who were present on the day of testing.

TABLE 2-3. Ethnicity of subjects in the normative sample

Ethnicity	Boys (n = 805)		Girls (n = 815)	
	Frequency	%	Frequency	%
White	616	76.5	619	76.0
Black	100	12.4	100	12.3
Asian	23	2.9	23	2.8
American Indian	21	2.6	26	3.2
Hispanic	18	2.2	16	2.0
Other	20	2.5	21	2.6
None reported	7	0.9	10	1.2

subjects drawn from western, midwestern, northeastern, and southern states.

Ethnicity. The MMPI-A normative sample demonstrates ethnic diversity as shown in Table 2-3. Most ethnic groups except Hispanics are well represented in the adolescent normative sample. Since this study required English-language reading ability at the sixth-grade level, those subjects who primarily read Spanish were not eligible. A Spanish version of the MMPI-A will be available in the future.

Age. The MMPI-A was designed for adolescents between the ages of 14 and 18 years (Table 2-4). Note that either the MMPI-A or MMPI-2 can be used with 18-year-olds. It is recommended that the MMPI-A be used for 18-year-olds still in high school and the adult version of the instrument, MMPI-2, be used for 18-year-olds in college or in other

TABLE 2-4. Ages of subjects in the normative sample

Age	Boys (n = 805)		Girls (n = 815)	
	Frequency	%	Frequency	%
14	193	24.0	174	21.3
15	207	25.7	231	28.3
16	228	28.3	202	24.8
17	135	16.7	163	20.0
18	42	5.2	45	5.5
	M = 15.54	SD = 1.17	M = 15.60	SD = 1.18

more adult roles. Although data from 12-and 13-year-olds were collected during the MMPI Restandardization Project, the younger subjects were not included in the norms for two primary reasons (Butcher et al., 1992). Our subjects under age 14 came from only two settings, a junior high school in the inner city of Minneapolis and a school in Virginia; thus, representativeness was limited. Furthermore, this limited sample of younger adolescents also appeared to have more difficulty reading and understanding the items, as reflected in their higher original F scores.

Grade. Since the decision was made to place the floor of the MMPI-A at age 14, most of the subjects in the normative sample were in ninth, tenth, eleventh, or twelfth grades, as noted in Table 2-5.

Current living situation. The living arrangements for the adolescent normative sample are described in Table 2-6. More than two-thirds of the normative sample reported living in homes with both mother and father. Adolescents living in blended families (i.e., with stepparents) are included in the "other" category.

Procedures Used for Clinical Data Collection

In each of the treatment facilities, Form TX was included in the standard admission assessment battery for all patients, with the adolescents and their parents invited to participate in the study by treatment staff. Informed consent was obtained from parents before including subjects in the study. The patients were administered Form TX of the MMPI in supervised sessions, usually individually, by staff within the first few weeks of admission. In a few instances, subjects completed

TABLE 2-5. Grades of subjects in the normative sample

	Boys (n = 805)		Girls (n = 815)	
Grade	Frequency	%	Frequency	%
Seventh	5	0.6	3	0.4
Eighth	57	7.1	64	7.9
Ninth	212	26.3	204	25.0
Tenth	238	29.6	235	28.8
Eleventh	206	25.6	184	22.6
Twelfth	87	10.8	124	15.2
None reported	0	0.0	1	0.1

TABLE 2-6. Current living situation of subjects in the normative sample

	Boys (n = 805)		Girls (n = 815)	
In home with	Frequency	%	Frequency	%
Mother and father	557	69.2	518	63.6
Mother only	191	23.7	229	28.1
Father only	28	3.5	34	4.2
Other	29	3.6	34	4.2

the MMPI in several short sessions rather than one long administration. Social reinforcement as well as tangible rewards, such as hospital privileges or candy, were used to elicit and maintain cooperation. These procedures were described by Williams and Butcher (1989a) in the study of the MMPI standard scales, although younger subjects ages 12 to 13 years were included in that study's sample. These younger subjects were excluded from the present sample when the decision was made to develop the MMPI-A for 14- to 18-year-olds.

The large majority of the clinical subjects (see Table 2-7) were drawn from inpatient alcohol and drug problem evaluation and treatment units (Fairview Deaconess Hospital and St. Mary's Hospital), followed by inpatient psychiatric units (Fairview Deaconess Hospital), special schools (Harrison Junior High School and the School Rehabilitation Center), and day treatment sites (Family Networks I and II). The special schools were public junior and senior high schools serving emotionally and behaviorally disturbed students in the Minneapolis School District.

In the special schools, the school psychologist reviewed the students' records for reading level to identify adolescents with at least a sixth-grade reading level (the level of reading required on Form TX), and then sent letters to parents offering a special psychological assessment

TABLE 2-7. Treatment settings of the clinical sample

Setting	Boys (n = 420)		Girls (n = 293)	
	Frequency	%	Frequency	%
Alcohol/drug units	299	71.2	163	55.6
Psychiatric units	67	16.0	96	32.8
Special schools	41	9.8	10	3.4
Day treatment	13	3.1	24	8.2

at no cost. The school psychologist and research assistants administered the TX version of the MMPI to groups of approximately four to five subjects in supervised testing sessions. The subjects were excused from classes in order to complete the testing and received praise, points, or candy as reinforcements for cooperation.

The Record Review Forms were completed by research assistants when the youngsters were discharged from the hospital or at the end of the school year. Day treatment and hospital staff completed DAB ratings after a period of observation and were instructed not to complete a DAB if they did not know the subject well enough. In the alcohol and drug problem units, the DAB was completed at the end of two weeks on the treatment units, because subjects did not stay long enough for assessment on the evaluation units. Some subjects do not have a DAB because they were discharged too soon or were not known well enough by staff. Since the schools did not have treatment counselors, the DAB data were not collected there.

The CBCL data were collected in the inpatient settings. The parents were given the CBCL by the staff when the adolescent was admitted and asked to complete it within a few days of the admission. The staff in the day treatment and special school settings were reluctant to request this information from parents, thus CBCLs were not collected at these sites. However, teachers in the special schools completed the TRF. As these procedures indicate, not all subjects in the clinical sample completed all measures. Table 2-1 presents information about the number of subjects completing each of the various measures in the clinical sample, with a comparison to the normative sample. Part of the variation in sample sizes is due to site-specific issues (e.g., the unavailability of counselors in the special school to complete the DAB). However, clinical subjects were somewhat less compliant with the procedures than the subjects in the normative sample. Thus, we changed the eligibility requirement of completion of all instruments in the core battery (i.e., Form TX, Biographical Information Form, and Life Events Form) used with the normative subjects to completion of just

TABLE 2-8. Ethnicity of subjects in the clinical sample

Ethnicity	Boys (n = 420)		Girls (n = 293)	
	Frequency	%	Frequency	%
White	316	75.2	225	76.8
Black	32	7.6	16	5.5
American Indian	32	7.6	16	5.5
Hispanic	7	1.7	0	0.0
Asian	0	0.0	2	0.7
Other	12	2.9	4	1.4
None reported	21	5.0	30	10.2

a valid (same criteria as used in the normative sample) Form TX in the clinical sample. Table 2-1 indicates the extent of the variations in sample sizes.

Description of the Adolescent Clinical Sample

Subjects in the adolescent clinical sample (420 boys and 293 girls) ranged in age from 14 through 18 years and were admitted to one of the treatment facilities described above during the period between November 1985 and March 1988. Although the majority of subjects came from the Minneapolis/St. Paul area, a number of them came from elsewhere in Minnesota and from several other states (Williams & Butcher, 1989a).

Demographic Characteristics of the Clinical Sample

Ethnicity. In ethnic composition (Table 2-8), the clinical sample is probably less representative of black adolescents in the general population than the MMPI-A normative sample because of the geographic area from which the sample was drawn. The sample shows a higher proportion of American Indians than in the general population, again reflecting the catchment area in which the Twin Cities treatment programs were located.

Age/grade. The age and grade distributions of the adolescent clinical sample are presented in Tables 2-9 and 2-10.

Current living situation. The information on current living situations

TABLE 2-9. Ages of subjects in the clinical sample

Age	Boys (n = 420)		Girls (n = 293)	
	Frequency	%	Frequency	%
14	58	13.8	54	18.4
15	102	24.3	91	31.1
16	130	31.0	77	26.3
17	106	25.2	58	19.8
18	24	5.7	13	4.4
	$M = 15.85$	$SD = 1.12$	$M = 15.61$	$SD = 1.13$

TABLE 2-10. Grades of subjects in the clinical sample

Grade	Boys (n = 420)		Girls (n = 293)	
	Frequency	%	Frequency	%
Seventh	12	2.9	7	2.4
Eighth	34	8.1	42	14.3
Ninth	109	26.0	64	21.8
Tenth	105	25.0	71	24.2
Eleventh	91	21.7	64	21.8
Twelfth	58	13.8	29	9.9
None reported	11	2.6	16	5.4

of subjects in the adolescent clinical sample presented in Table 2-11 is revealing when compared with Table 2-6, which presents the same information for the normative sample. Although the majority of the adolescents in the MMPI-A normative sample live with both parents, youngsters from the clinical samples tend to come from single-parent families. This finding is consistent with results that have been reported in the adolescent problem literature showing an association between psychopathology in children and adolescents and family disruption (Bloom, Asher, & White, 1978).

Summary of Methods

The MMPI Restandardization Project used several samples, measures, and procedures in developing the MMPI-A. An experimental 704-item booklet, Form TX, was administered to adolescents in school and clinical settings. The standard core battery administered to all subjects included Form TX as well as a Biographical Information Form and a

TABLE 2-11. Current living situation of subjects in the clinical sample

In home with	Boys (n = 420)		Girls (n = 293)	
	Frequency	%	Frequency	%
Mother and father	137	32.6	95	32.4
Mother only	186	44.3	101	34.5
Father only	39	9.3	29	9.9
Other	58	13.8	68	23.2

Life Events Form. Information from this battery provided descriptions of the demographic characteristics of the normative and clinical samples used to develop the MMPI-A Content Scales.

Normative subjects were drawn from schools in eight states located in different regions of the country. Adolescents ages 14-18, in seventh to twelfth grades, were included (805 boys, 815 girls). The normative sample was ethnically diverse, and the majority of subjects reported living at home with both parents. This chapter highlighted the procedures used to collect these data.

The clinical subjects were sampled from several treatment facilities in the Twin Cities area. This sample of 420 boys and 293 girls was predominantly seen in alcohol and other drug problem inpatient evaluation and treatment units. A smaller number of clinical subjects came from psychiatric inpatient units, special schools, and day treatment centers. Like the normative sample, the clinical sample ranged in age from 14 to 18 years (seventh to twelfth grades). The clinical subjects also were ethnically diverse, although more representative of local ethnic group distribution. Subjects in the clinical sample were more likely to come from disrupted homes than were the normative subjects. In addition to the core battery, other assessment information was collected for the clinical subjects, including parent or treatment staff ratings, record reviews, and other self-reports. The normative and clinical samples, along with the measures and procedures described in this chapter, were used in our efforts to develop the MMPI-A Content Scales presented in the remainder of this monograph.

Chapter 3

Developmental Strategy for the MMPI-A Content Scales

The developmental strategy for the MMPI-A Content Scales evolved from a rich heritage of research over the last 60 years. Work on the original MMPI in the 1930s and 1940s stimulated interest in objective personality scale construction. The efforts of Jerry Wiggins and his colleagues provided an original approach to MMPI scale construction and interpretation with the development of the widely used Wiggins Content Scales for the MMPI (Wiggins, 1966, 1969; Wiggins, Goldberg, & Appelbaum, 1971; Wiggins & Vollmar, 1959). Butcher et al. (1990) summarize the history of personality scale construction, using a classification scheme for the various construction strategies previously presented by Burisch (1984):

1. the empirical or external approach (the method used in constructing the original MMPI standard scales)

2. the factor-analytic or inductive approach

3. the deductive approach (includes theoretical, rational, and construct-oriented methods)

Development of the MMPI-A Content Scales most closely approximated the deductive approach, for it included a combination of rational and statistical steps. Multistage, multimethod procedures similar to those used in developing the MMPI-2 Content Scales (Butcher et al., 1990) were used with the MMPI-A Content Scales. Because of these parallels in their development, and because the MMPI-2 Content Scales provided the core for many of the MMPI-A Content Scales, we will review briefly the development of the MMPI-2 Content Scales. A more detailed description of this work is available in Butcher et al. (1990).

Development of MMPI-2 Content Scales

The five-stage process of developing the MMPI-2 Content Scales began with a rational identification of content areas in Form AX, the experimental adult MMPI booklet developed by the MMPI Restandardization Committee. A total of 22 content categories were selected for further study in Stage I, Step 1. In Step 2, three independent raters rationally grouped the 704 Form AX items into these 22 categories. This was followed by a group consensus meeting to determine which items would be kept. One of the 22 categories was dropped at this point because too few of the items available in Form AX were relevant to its content domain. This left 21 provisional content scales for the statistical Stage II.

Stage II was the first statistical verification of the rationally derived provisional content scales using item-scale correlations and coefficient alphas, a measure of internal consistency (Cronbach, 1951), to verify item-scale memberships. Several different samples, both normal and clinical, separated by gender, were used in these analyses. Any rationally selected items that produced Pearson product-moment correlation coefficients substantially lower than the majority of the items on that scale and the deletion of which would increase the scale's coefficient alpha by at least two points (e.g., .78 rises to .80) were deleted from scale membership. Similarly, items originally left out of provisional scales were added when their correlations with the scale reached or exceeded .50 in the validation sample and .45 in a cross-validation sample. The next two stages were designed to ensure that only those items genuinely related to the core content areas were retained.

Stage III involved a final rational review, necessitated by the additions and deletions that occurred during Stage II. A few scale names were changed because their content domains had changed with the addition or deletion of items. Any items that met the statistical criteria of Stage II but had content inappropriate for the construct measured by the scale were dropped from the scale. Finally, item overlap was inspected and largely eliminated.

The final statistical refinement of Stage IV identified for elimination from scale membership any item that correlated more highly with a scale other than the one to which it originally had been assigned. Uniform T scores, consistent with the MMPI-2 standard scores (Butcher et al., 1989), were then derived for the MMPI-2 Content Scales. In the final stage, rational descriptions were written for each of the MMPI-2 Content Scales. The 15 MMPI-2 Content Scales listed in Table 3-1 resulted from these procedures.

Figure 3-1
Developmental stages of MMPI-A Content Scales

Stage I
Determination of initial content scales
Step 1 Identification of MMPI-2 Content Scales developmentally inappropriate for adolescents
2 Identification of MMPI-2 Content Scale items included in Form TX
3 Independent rater identification and addition of Form TX items not on MMPI-2 Content Scales
4 Independent rater identification and deletion of MMPI-2 Content Scale items developmentally inappropriate as measures of personality psycho-pathology in adolescents
5 Independent rater identification of potential adolescent-specific content scales
6 Group consensus on list for initial content scales
7 Elimination of most item overlap

Stage II
Statistical verification of initial content scales
Step 8 Identification and deletion of items not statistically related to scales
9 Identification and addition of items correlated with scales but not previously selected
10 Determination of reliability coefficients of initial scales
11 Determination of validity coefficients of initial scales
12 Deletion of scales without adequate reliability and validity

---

Stage III
Final rational review
Step 13 Examination of the changed content dimensions
14 Rational and statistical development of conduct problems scale following Steps 5 through 13

Stage IV
Final statistical refinement
Step 15 Elimination of items more highly correlated with other scales
16 Computation of final reliability coefficients
17 Derivation of uniform T scores for content scales
18 Computation of final validity coefficients

Stage V
Descriptions for scales
Step 19 Items inspected and content-based description written for each scale
20 Narrative integration of content-based and empirically derived descriptors

Development of Content Scales for Adolescents

Given that recent studies have documented the usefulness and validity of the MMPI-2 Content Scales with adults (e.g., Ben-Porath, Butcher, & Graham, 1991; Egeland, Erickson, Butcher, & Ben-Porath, 1991; Hjemboe & Butcher, 1991; Lilienfeld, 1991; Walsh et al., 1991), we decided to adapt most of the scales for use with adolescents and to develop several additional scales specifically for use with younger individuals. Figure 3-1 presents the multistage, multimethod procedures used for the development of the MMPI-A Content Scales. As with the MMPI-2 Content Scales, both rational and statistical steps were pursued in stages.

Stage I involved the determination of our initial or provisional content scales. Our first step was to examine the list of MMPI-2 Content Scales to determine if any of these constructs seemed developmentally inappropriate for adolescents. The Work Interference Scale was dropped at Step 1 because it was seen as less relevant for adolescents. In fact, many of its items had been added to the adult Form AX, but not to the adolescent Form TX. Therefore, the item content to develop this scale was not available on Form TX. We also knew that we would be replacing the Work Interference Scale with one measuring school problems, since several school-related items had been added to Form TX when the work-related items were added to Form AX.

Next, we determined how many items from the MMPI-2 Content Scales were contained in the Form TX booklet (Table 3-1). Form TX contained all of the items from some MMPI-2 Content Scales (e.g., Anxiety and Antisocial Practices), and other MMPI-2 Content Scales lost several items (e.g., Obsessiveness, a relatively short MMPI-2 scale, dropped from 16 items to 12 items on Form TX; Type A Behavior dropped from 19 items on MMPI-2 to 12 items on Form TX).

However, it was apparent at Stage I that some of the adolescent-specific item content available in Form TX might be added to the MMPI-2 Content Scales to create adolescent versions of these scales. In Step 3, three of the authors (Williams, Butcher, & Ben-Porath) independently rated Form TX items and added them to relevant provisional content domains. For example, an adolescent-specific item stating, "I have missed a lot of school in my life because of sickness," was added to Health Concerns. The Family Problems Scale gained the most items because Form TX had been expanded to address adolescent-specific family issues. The additions included items such as the following:

I have spent nights away from home when my parents did not know where I was.

TABLE 3-1. MMPI-2 Content Scales used to evaluate content domains on Form TX (Stage I of developmental strategy)

MMPI-2 Content Scales	Number of items on MMPI-2	Number of items on TX	Decision
Anxiety	23	23	Retain
Fears	23	22	Retain
Obsessiveness	16	12	Retain
Depression	33	26	Retain
Health Concerns	36	36	Retain
Bizarre Mentation	24	23	Retain
Anger	16	11	Retain
Cynicism	23	22	Retain
Antisocial Practices	22	22	Retain
Type A Behavior	19	12	Retain
Low Self-Esteem	24	21	Retain
Social Discomfort	24	22	Retain
Family Problems	25	21	Retain
Work Interference	33	—	Replace
Negative Treatment Indicators	26	21	Retain

I cannot wait for the day when I can leave home for good.

My parents do not like my friends.

In Step 4, raters independently identified and deleted any content scale items judged developmentally inappropriate as measures of personality or psychopathology in adolescents. The relatively few items that were deleted included one on Health Concerns, "I have never had any breaking out on my skin that has worried me," which was dropped because of adolescents' preoccupation with acne. Another item from the Anxiety Scale, "I worry over money and business," did not seem to be as relevant a worry for adolescents as it was for adults.

By the conclusion of Step 4, we had a list of provisional content scales derived from the MMPI-2 list. However, we also had a substantial number of adolescent-specific items from Form TX that were not appropriate for any of the MMPI-2 Content Scales. Therefore, in our next step, the independent raters identified potential adolescent-specific content domains: eating problems, sexual issues, adolescent turmoil, peer group orientation, identity concerns, alienation, low aspirations, and school problems (Table 3-2). Some of these content domains did not last long. For example, there were too few items to develop an eating problems scale, so it was eliminated by group consensus in Step 6. We also agreed that items grouped under sexual

TABLE 3-2. Provisional adolescent-specific content domains on Form TX (Stage I of developmental strategy)

Content domain	Outcome
Eating problems	Dropped Stage I: too few items; retained for item-level indicator
Sexual issues	Dropped Stage I: group consensus
Adolescent turmoil	Dropped Stage II: low reliability
Peer group orientation	Dropped Stage II: low reliability
Identity concerns	Dropped Stage II: low reliability
Alienation	MMPI-A Content Scale
Low aspirations	MMPI-A Content Scale
School problems	MMPI-A Content Scale

issues really did not form a cohesive scale, nor did the adolescent turmoil items. Therefore, both of these domains also were dropped.

In Step 7, the last step in Stage I, most item overlap was eliminated. Awareness of the problems of the high prevalence of Scale 4 responding in adolescent settings led us to be sensitive to problems with heterogeneous item content in measures of acting out. Elevations on Scale 4, for example, can occur because of problems in a number of content domains, including family discord, authority problems, and alienation. This could explain some of the difficulty in interpreting MMPIs from adolescents. We were very careful in developing the MMPI-A Content Scales that assess acting-out problems to ensure that these separate scales had no item overlap. All item overlap was eliminated from Antisocial Practices (replaced by Conduct Problems, in Stage III), School Problems, and Family Problems. Table 3-3 shows remaining item overlap. Negative Treatment Indicators (A-trt) has the most item overlap (14 items) with other MMPI-A Content Scales because its underlying construct is related to several indices of psychopathology that are measured by the other scales. Next is Low Self-Esteem (A-lse), which shares four items with three other MMPI-A Content Scales—again, because of construct overlap (i.e., low self-esteem is conceptually related to anxiety, depression, and alienation). Most of the 14 other MMPI-A Content Scales overlap with each other by only one or two items. Bizarre Mentation (A-biz) shares no items with any of the other MMPI-A Content Scales.

Stage II in the MMPI-A Content Scales' development was very similar to the second stage for the MMPI-2 Content Scales, involving statistical verification of the provisional content scales. Item-scale correlations and coefficient alphas for the provisional scales were computed to determine if the rationally selected items were statistically related to

TABLE 3-3. Item overlap of MMPI-A Content Scales

	A-anx	A-obs	A-dep	A-hea	A-biz	A-ang	A-cyn	A-aln	A-con	A-lse	A-las	A-sod	A-fam	A-sch	A-trt
A-anx	X														
A-obs	1	X													
A-dep			X												
A-hea				X											
A-biz					X										
A-ang						X									
A-cyn			1				X								
A-aln			1			1	1	X							
A-con								1	X						
A-lse	1		2				1	1	1	X					
A-las								1		1	X				
A-sod								1				X			
A-fam								1					X		
A-sch				1							1			X	
A-trt		2	3				1	3	1	2	2				X

the scales. We lost two additional domains, peer group orientation and identity concerns, at this stage because of low reliability. In both cases, the provisional scales' coefficient alpha failed to exceed .50 for at least one gender in both the normative and clinical samples. But, as Table 3-2 reveals, three of our adolescent-specific content domains were retained as MMPI-A Content Scales, having survived all the stages of development.

Two of the content domains that we were interested in including had somewhat lower reliability coefficients than the others. Type A and Low Aspirations had reliability coefficients in the .55 to .65 range. Thus, in an additional step, we calculated and examined validity coefficients for Type A and Low Aspirations before deciding these domains' eventual fate. These validity analyses followed the methods described in Chapter 5, using the same criterion measures and analyses. The Type A Scale was dropped when Step 11 revealed no correlates from either the provisional normative or clinical samples for boys or girls. There were just too few items on Form TX to develop a reliable and valid Type A scale for adolescents. On the other hand, Low Aspirations demonstrated adequate validity in our provisional samples (see Chapter 5, Table 5-10, for the obtained correlates from the final normative and clinical samples for A-las). This scale was retained.

Stage III, like the analogous stage in the development of the MMPI-2 Content Scales, was the final rational review of our provisional scales. The changes in item content in the various domains were examined to ensure that scale names were accurate. The most significant outcome at Stage III was the development of an alternative Antisocial Practices Scale (Step 14). Preliminary validity analyses of the initial content scales (Step 11) revealed disappointingly few correlates for the Antisocial Practices Scale (ASP) in our adolescent samples (Table 3-4). The validity correlates for ASP, which were calculated earlier in our developmental work, were derived from provisional normative and clinical samples (i.e., the age range had not been set nor was data collection completed for the normative boys). However, these slight sampling differences were unlikely to account for the relatively poor performance of ASP. The richness of our criterion measures for assessing acting out, plus the validity established for Scale 4 using the same criterion measures and samples (Williams & Butcher, 1989a), contributed to our disappointment in ASP, and led to the development of the Adolescent Conduct Problems (A-con) Scale. Using the 704 Form TX items, Williams identified a new content domain to assess conduct problems in adolescents, without using the items in the adult ASP Content Scale to define this domain, in a procedure similar to Step 5. Development of the A-con Scale then followed the same path as the other scales (Figure 3-1). A comparison of the correlates

TABLE 3-4. Correlates for the ASP Scales for the provisional normative and clinical boys and girls (Step 11)

Source	Scale or item	Provisional normative sample		Provisional clinical sample	
		Boys ($n = 590$)	Girls ($n = 845$)	Boys ($n = 407$)	Girls ($n = 305$)
BIO	Number of school problems	NS	.24	NS	NS
BIO	Marks in school	NS	.19	NS	NS
LE	Increase in disagreements with parent(s)	NS	.20	NS	NS
LE	Used drugs or alcohol	.18	.19	NS	NS
LE	Court appearance	NS	NS	NS	.27
LE	Arrested for stealing	NS	NS	NS	.18
LE	Suspended from school	NS	NS	NS	.18
CBCL	Delinquent	NA	NA	.22	NS
CBCL	Social Competence: Social	NA	NA	NS	−.19
RR	Experience with amphetamines	NA	NA	.19	NS

Note: BIO refers to Biographical Information Form, LE to Life Events Form, CBCL to Child Behavior Checklist, and RR to Record Review. All correlations (r) are Pearson product-moment correlation coefficients with $p \leq .0005$ and an absolute magnitude $\geq .18$. NS (not significant) indicates the correlate did not reach these significance criteria. NA (not available) indicates that these measures were not collected for the normative subjects.

for ASP (Table 3-4) with the correlates obtained for the A-con Scale (Chapter 5, Table 5-8) confirmed our belief that we could develop a better content scale for assessing acting-out behaviors in adolescents. Only 7 of the 23 items in the final A-con Scale overlapped with ASP content.

Stage IV involved the final statistical refinement of the MMPI-A Content Scales and Stage V the development of their final descriptions. As in the MMPI-2 Content Scales' development, we eliminated items that were more highly correlated with other scales, computed the final reliability coefficients (Chapter 4), derived uniform T scores for the MMPI-A Content Scales (Chapter 4), and computed the final validity coefficients (Chapter 5). Table 3-5 describes the final list of MMPI-A Content Scales. None of these scales overlaps exactly with the parent MMPI-2 Content Scale. For this reason, we thought it important to distinguish between the adult and adolescent versions of the scales by inserting the capital letter A in front of the abbreviations, in lowercase, for the adolescent scales' names (e.g., A-anx) compared with the adult versions (ANX).

Although an adolescent counterpart of the MMPI-2 Fears (FRS) Scale was developed, it was dropped. Much of its item content was unique to A-frs and did not appear on any other MMPI-A scale. Because of the desire to shorten the MMPI-A and because the instrument contained several other anxiety-related scales, the items unique to the A-frs Scale were deleted from the MMPI-A booklet (Butcher et al., 1992).

Three new adolescent-specific content scales (i.e., Adolescent-Alienation, Adolescent-Low Aspirations, Adolescent-School Problems) were added. The original Antisocial Practices (ASP) content changed so much that it was renamed Adolescent-Conduct Problems (A-con). The Adolescent-Family Problems (A-fam) Scale increased its item content significantly compared with the original FAM scale. Content-based descriptions of all 15 scales (Step 19) are presented in Table 3-5. The results of Step 20, the narrative summaries of the content-based and empirically derived descriptors, are presented scale by scale in Chapter 6. Appendix D presents the item composition of the MMPI-A Content Scales. The next chapter details the psychometric properties of these new scales.

TABLE 3-5. Descriptions of MMPI-A Content Scales

A-anx (Adolescent-Anxiety)

Number of items on A-anx/ANX: 21/31
Items in common with adult ANX: 20
A-anx content: Adolescents who score high on A-anx report many symptoms of anxiety, including tension, frequent worrying, difficulties sleeping (e.g., nightmares, disturbed sleep, difficulty falling asleep). They report problems with concentration, confusion, and inability to stay on task. Life is a strain for them and they believe that their difficulties are insurmountable. High scorers worry about losing their minds and feel that something dreadful is about to happen. They appear aware of their problems and how they differ from others.

A-obs (Adolescent-Obsessiveness)

Number of items on A-obs/OBS: 15/16
Items in common with adult OBS: 12
A-obs content: Adolescent high scorers on A-obs report worrying beyond reason, often over trivial matters. They may ruminate about "bad words" or counting unimportant items. They have times when they are unable to sleep because of their worries. They report great difficulty making decisions and frequently dread having to make changes in their lives. They report that others sometimes lose patience with them. They are often regretful about things they may have said or done.

A-dep (Adolescent-Depression)

Number of items on A-dep/DEP: 26/33
Items in common with adult DEP: 25
A-dep content: Adolescents who score high on A-dep report many symptoms of depression. Frequent crying spells and fatigue are problems. They feel that others are happier and that they are dissatisfied with their lives. They have many self-deprecative thoughts, including beliefs that they have not lived the right kind of life, feelings of uselessness, and beliefs that they are condemned and their sins unpardonable. Their future seems hopeless and life is not worthwhile and is uninteresting. Most of the time they report feeling blue and wishing they were dead. Suicidal ideations are possible. They report loneliness even when with other people. Their future seems too uncertain for them to make serious plans and they have periods when they are unable to "get going." A sense of hopelessness, not caring what happens, and an inclination to take things hard are other characteristics.

A-hea (Adolescent-Health Concerns)

Number of items on A-hea/HEA: 37/36
Items in common with adult HEA: 34
A-hea content: Adolescents with high scores on A-hea report numerous physical problems that interfere with their enjoyment of after-school activities and that contribute to significant school absence. They may report that their physical health is worse than their friends'. Their physical complaints cross several body systems. Included are gastrointestinal problems (e.g., constipation, nausea and vomiting, stomach trouble), neurological problems (e.g., numbness, convulsions, fainting and dizzy spells, paralysis), sensory problems (e.g., hearing difficulty, poor eyesight), cardiovascular symptoms (e.g., heart or chest pain), skin problems, pain (e.g., headaches, neck pain), and respiratory problems. High scorers report worrying about their health and feeling that their problems would disappear if only their health would improve.

A-aln (Adolescent-Alienation)

Number of items on A-aln: 20
A-aln content: High scorers on A-aln, one of the adolescent-specific content scales, report considerable emotional distance from others. They believe that they are getting a raw deal from life and that no one cares about or understands them. They do not believe that they are liked by others, nor do they get along with others. They have no one, including parents or close friends, who understands them. They feel that others are out to get them and are unkind to them. They do not believe they have as much fun as other adolescents, and would prefer living all alone in a cabin in the woods. They have difficulty self-disclosing and report feeling awkward when having to talk in a group. They do not appreciate hearing others give their opinions. They do not believe others are sympathetic and feel that other people often block their attempts at success.

A-biz (Adolescent-Bizarre Mentation)

Number of items on A-biz/BIZ: 19/24
Items in common with adult BIZ: 17
A-biz content: Adolescents scoring high on A-biz report very strange thoughts and experiences, including possible auditory, visual, and olfactory hallucinations. They characterize their experiences as strange and unusual, and believe there is something wrong with their minds. Paranoid ideation (i.e., the belief that they are being plotted against or someone is trying to poison them) may also be reported. They may believe that others are trying to steal their thoughts and ideas or control their minds, perhaps through hypnosis. They may believe that evil spirits or ghosts possess or influence them.

A-ang (Adolescent-Anger)

Number of items on A-ang/ANG: 17/16
Items in common with adult ANG: 11
A-ang content: Adolescents with high scores on A-ang report considerable anger control problems. They often feel like swearing, smashing things, or starting a fistfight, and frequently get into trouble for breaking or destroying things. They report having considerable problems with irritability and impatience with others. They have been told that they throw temper tantrums to get their way. They indicate that they are hotheaded and often have to yell in order to make a point. Occasionally they get into fights, especially when drinking. They do not like others to hurry them or to get ahead of them in a line.

A-cyn (Adolescent-Cynicism)

Number of items on A-cyn/CYN: 22/23
Items in common with adult CYN: 21
A-cyn content: Misanthropic attitudes are held by adolescents scoring high on A-cyn. They believe that others are out to get them and will use unfair means to gain an advantage. They look for hidden motives whenever someone does something nice for them. They believe that it is safer to trust nobody because people make friends in order to use them. They see others as inwardly disliking helping another person, and they are on guard when people seem friendlier than they expect. They feel misunderstood by others, and see others as very jealous of them.

TABLE 3-5. Descriptions of MMPI-A Content Scales (continued)

A-con (Adolescent-Conduct Problems)

Number of items on A-con/ASP: 23/22
Items in common with adult ASP: 7
A-con content: Adolescents scoring high on A-con report a number of different behavioral problems, including stealing, shoplifting, lying, breaking or destroying things, being disrespectful, swearing, and being oppositional. Their peer group is often in trouble and frequently talks them into doing things they know they should not do. At times they try to make other people afraid of them, just for the fun of it. They are entertained by another's criminal behavior, and do not blame people for taking advantage of others. They admit to doing bad things in the past that they cannot tell anybody about.

A-lse (Adolescent-Low Self-Esteem)

Number of items on A-lse/LSE: 18/24
Items in common with adult LSE: 18
A-lse content: Adolescents with high A-lse scores have very negative opinions of themselves, including being unattractive, lacking self-confidence, feeling useless, having little ability, having several faults, and not being able to do anything well. They are likely to yield to others' pressure, changing their minds or giving up in arguments. They tend to let other people take charge when problems have to be solved, and do not feel that they are capable of planning their own future. They become uncomfortable when others say nice things about them. They may get confused and forgetful.

A-las (Adolescent-Low Aspirations)

Number of items on A-las: 16
A-las content: High scorers on A-las, an adolescent-specific scale, are disinterested in being successful. They do not like to study and read about things, dislike science, dislike lectures on serious topics, and prefer work that allows them to be careless. They do not expect to be successful. They avoid newspaper editorials and believe that the comic strips are the only interesting part of the newspaper. They report difficulty starting things and quickly give up when things go wrong. They let other people solve problems and they avoid facing difficulties. They believe that others block their success. Others also tell them that they are lazy.

A-sod (Adolescent-Social Discomfort)

Number of items on A-sod/SOD: 24/24
Items in common with Adult SOD: 21
A-sod content: Adolescents with high scores on A-sod find it very difficult to be around others. They report being shy and much prefer to be alone. They dislike having people around them and frequently avoid others. They do not like parties, crowds, dances, or other social gatherings. They will not speak unless first spoken to, and others indicate that it is hard to get to know them. They have difficulty making friends and do not like to meet strangers.

A-fam (Adolescent-Family Problems)

Number of items on A-fam/FAM: 35/25
Items in common with adult FAM: 15
A-fam content: Adolescents with high A-fam scores report considerable problems with their parents and other family members. Discord, jealousy, faultfinding, anger, beatings, serious disagreements, lack of love and understanding, and limited communication characterize these families. These adolescents do not believe they can count on their families in times of trouble. They wish for the day when they are able to leave their homes. They feel their parents frequently punish them without cause, and treat them more like children. They report that their parents dislike their peer group.

A-sch (Adolescent-School Problems)

Number of items on A-sch: 20
A-sch content: Numerous difficulties in school characterize adolescents scoring high on A-sch, another of the adolescent-specific content scales. Poor grades, suspension, truancy, negative attitudes toward teachers, and dislike of school are characteristic of high scorers. The only pleasant aspect of school for youth high on A-sch is their friends. They do not participate in school activities or sports. They believe that school is a waste of time. They have been told that they are lazy. They report frequent boredom and sleepiness at school. Some of these individuals may report being afraid to go to school.

A-trt (Adolescent-Negative Treatment Indicators)

Number of items on A-trt/TRT: 26/26
Items in common with adult TRT: 21
A-trt content: High scorers on A-trt indicate negative attitudes toward doctors and mental health professionals. They do not believe that others are capable of understanding them or that others care about what happens to them. They are unwilling to take charge and face their problems or difficulties. They report several faults and bad habits that they feel are insurmountable. They do not feel they can plan their own futures. They will not assume responsibility for negative things in their lives. They also report great unwillingness to discuss their problems with others and indicate that there are some issues that they would never be able to share with anyone. They report being nervous when others ask them personal questions and have many secrets they feel are best kept to themselves.

Chapter 4

Psychometric Characteristics of the MMPI-A Content Scales

A fundamental requirement for developing and using psychometric measures is that they yield reliable information. With multiscale measures such as the MMPI-A, proper standardization is also of vital importance to assure that meaningful comparisons can be made of scores obtained by the same client on different scales. In this chapter, we present data documenting the MMPI-A Content Scales' psychometric characteristics, including their internal consistency and test-retest reliability, descriptive statistics on the scales' functioning in normal and clinical samples, and correlational statistics pertaining to interrelatedness within the MMPI-A Content Scales and between the MMPI-A Content Scales and other MMPI scales, such as the standard scales and the Wiggins Content Scales.

Reliability

Following our initial work with the MMPI-2 Content Scales, the MMPI-A Content Scales were developed with the goal of maximizing their internal consistency. As described in Chapter 3, this was achieved by deleting items that attenuated a scale's internal consistency and adding items that correlated with a scale both statistically and conceptually. Table 4-1 presents Cronbach's (1951) alpha, a measure of reliability based on internal consistency, for the MMPI-A Content Scales. Alpha coefficients were computed separately for boys and girls in the clinical and normative samples described in Chapter 2.

For the most part, the internal consistencies of the MMPI-A Content Scales fall in the .70s and .80s. On average, internal consistency for girls is higher than for boys. The mean alpha for clinical girls is .80, the mean for normative girls is .76, and the respective means for boys were .76 and .74. Overall, the MMPI-A Content Scales demonstrate adequate internal consistency, though these statistics are gener-

Table 4-1. Reliability of the MMPI-A Content Scales

| Scales | Clinical sample Cronbach's alpha | | Normative sample Cronbach's alpha | | r_{tt} [a] |
	Boys ($n = 420$)	Girls ($n = 293$)	Boys ($n = 805$)	Girls ($n = 815$)	($n = 154$)
A-anx	.80	.86	.76	.80	.81
A-obs	.76	.80	.72	.72	.70
A-dep	.83	.89	.80	.83	.82
A-hea	.78	.85	.81	.82	.76
A-biz	.73	.76	.75	.75	.68
A-ang	.75	.79	.69	.66	.72
A-cyn	.78	.83	.79	.81	.73
A-aln	.72	.75	.69	.75	.62
A-con	.74	.79	.72	.72	.62
A-lse	.73	.80	.71	.75	.78
A-las	.63	.63	.55	.59	.66
A-sod	.78	.85	.77	.78	.76
A-fam	.82	.82	.81	.82	.82
A-sch	.70	.74	.69	.69	.64
A-trt	.77	.80	.72	.75	.68

[a]One-week test-retest of normative sample, boys and girls combined.

ally lower than those found for the MMPI-2 Content Scales in adults. This parallels the pattern found in the MMPI-A and MMPI-2 standard scales (Butcher et al., 1992), and is likely a function of the increased noise and resultant decreased precision that characterizes the psychometric assessment of adolescents. Of particular note is the low level of internal consistency found for the Low Aspirations Scale. Based on internal consistency information alone, we were inclined to discard this scale; however, we decided to include it in the validity analyses before making a final decision (see Chapter 3). Since the scale was found to have meaningful correlates despite restricted internal consistency (see Chapter 5), and, as indicated later in this chapter, this scale has relatively low correlations with other MMPI-A Content Scales (beyond what would be expected as a function of its attenuated reliability), we decided against removing it.

Table 4-1 also includes information on the MMPI-A Content Scales' test-retest reliability. These data are based on a subset of 154 of the normative subjects who retook Form TX within a one-week interval. The data provided by boys and girls were combined, because only 45 boys completed the retest. On average, the MMPI-A Content Scales' test-retest reliability is .73, slightly lower than their internal consistency. This, in part, may be the result of the instability that characterizes adolescents, which has been noted since the time of G. Stanley Hall. The test-retest reliability of the MMPI-A Content Scales is simi-

TABLE 4-2. Reliability of the Wiggins Content Scales

Scales	Clinical sample Cronbach's alpha		Normative sample Cronbach's alpha		r_{tt} [a]
	Boys ($n = 420$)	Girls ($n = 293$)	Boys ($n = 805$)	Girls ($n = 815$)	($n = 154$)
HEA	.67	.74	.68	.65	.72
DEP	.84	.89	.80	.84	.81
ORG	.78	.85	.81	.80	.72
FAM	.68	.67	.65	.69	.79
AUT	.68	.76	.70	.70	.69
FEM	.53	.55	.48	.51	.84
REL	.72	.70	.75	.72	.84
HOS	.80	.81	.75	.74	.63
MOR	.82	.87	.78	.80	.84
PHO	.71	.76	.74	.69	.76
PSY	.84	.86	.83	.83	.73
HYP	.71	.73	.72	.67	.72
SOC	.74	.84	.75	.78	.76

[a]One-week test-retest of normative sample, boys and girls combined.

lar in magnitude to that of other self-report measures designed to assess psychopathology in adolescents (e.g., the Youth Self-Report Form; Achenbach & Edelbrock, 1987).

In general, the internal consistency of the MMPI-A Content Scales is higher than that of the MMPI-A standard scales as reported by Butcher et al. (1992). Their test-retest reliability is of the same magnitude. Another meaningful comparison group for the MMPI-A Content Scales is the Wiggins (1969) Content Scales. Since all of the subjects completed the experimental Form TX, both sets of content scales could be computed and evaluated. Table 4-2 provides reliability data on the Wiggins Content Scales for girls and boys in the clinical and normative samples.

Tables 4-1 and 4-2 show considerable comparability in the reliability of the MMPI-A Content Scales and the Wiggins Content Scales. Mean alpha coefficients on the Wiggins Content Scales for clinical boys and girls were .74 and .79, respectively; means for the normative boys and girls were both .73. Examination of individual scales measuring comparable areas reveals some cases in which the MMPI-A Content Scales outperform the Wiggins Content Scales, such as Health Concerns and Family Problems (the latter contains many new items written specifically for adolescents), and one case where the Wiggins Psychoticism Scale outperforms the MMPI-A Bizarre Mentation Scale (perhaps in part because the latter is made up of less frequently endorsed items than the former). Overall, the two sets of scales are quite comparable in their level of internal consistency. With respect to test-retest reliability, the mean for the Wiggins Content Scales, .76, is slightly higher than that for the MMPI-A Content Scales. This difference does not reach a level that would suggest any meaningful difference in reliability between the two sets.

Overall, the MMPI-A Content Scales' reliability is comparable to the reliability of other scales developed for use with adolescents. In general, the reliability of psychometric testing with adolescents is lower than that found with adults. This suggests the need for test interpreters to realize that a wider confidence interval is needed around a given adolescent's scale score when reporting the results of an MMPI-A evaluation. With this population, we should expect the individual's true score on any given scale to fluctuate within a wider range surrounding the observed score than is the case with adults. These interpretive cautions notwithstanding, the validity data presented in Chapter 5 illustrate that despite the slight attenuation in reliability, meaningful and statistically significant extratest correlates for the MMPI-A Content Scales are plentiful. Thus, given the requisite amount of interpretive caution, the MMPI-A Content Scales can be used to generate meaningful and clinically significant interpretive hypotheses.

Descriptive Statistics

Two types of descriptive statistics for the MMPI-A Content Scales are provided below. The scales' skewness, kurtosis, and percentile equivalents of the T scores will be presented to illustrate the need for, and selected effects of, the use of uniform T scores. Next, we will present the scale means and standard deviations to enable future investigators to compare their samples with the clinical and normative samples used in the development of the MMPI-A Content Scales.

Uniform T Scores

Uniform T scores were developed by Auke Tellegen as part of the MMPI Restandardization Project for adults to correct a problem that had characterized the original instrument's linear T scores. As discussed by Tellegen and Ben-Porath (in press), linear T scores retain the shape of the distribution of raw scores. To the extent that scales have different raw score distributions, this will lead to a lack of percentile equivalence for the same T scores across different scales. Previous researchers chose to transform adolescent MMPI raw scores into normalized T scores by adjusting the distribution of each scale to fit a normal distribution (see Colligan & Offord, 1989; Gottesman et al., 1987). However, the problem of differential distributions was solved at the cost of considerable deviation from the characteristically skewed nature of MMPI scale distributions, which results in considerable change in the configural relations (i.e., code types) among scales and the attenuation of scores at higher levels of elevation. Uniform T scores adjust each scale's distribution to fit a composite distribution, which is based on the mean distribution of the MMPI-2 normative sample on the non-K-corrected eight clinical scales. Thus, in the MMPI-2, the problem of lack of percentile equivalence was solved while the overall skewed nature of the distributions was retained.

In developing uniform T scores for the MMPI-A scales, the Restandardization Committee decided to use as the composite for adjusting each individual scale the same target distribution used by Tellegen in developing the MMPI-2 uniform T scores. This was done in order to ensure percentile equivalence across the two forms (MMPI-2 and MMPI-A) so that an individual's scores on both versions could be compared directly (e.g., in cases where a 17- or 18-year-old is administered the MMPI-A at one time, and then a year later completes the MMPI-2). Table 4-3 provides data illustrating the need for, and the effect of the development of, uniform T scores for the MMPI-A.

As seen in Table 4-3, the range of skewness of linear T scores in the MMPI-A normative sample is .967 for boys and .998 for girls. In contrast, for the uniform T scores the corresponding ranges of skewness are .174 and .119, respectively. Thus, the uniform transformation has succeeded in reducing considerably any discrepancies in scale skewness. Of note is the discrepancy between the mean skewness for linear and uniform T scores. For boys, the mean skewness for linear T scores is .257, and for uniform T scores it is .758. For girls, the respective figures are .262 and .749. The reason for this discrepancy is the decision, mentioned above, to calibrate MMPI-A uniform T scores to MMPI-2 uniform T scores, and, in fact, the means for the uniform T scores are the same as those found in the MMPI-2 clinical and content scales (Butcher et al., 1989, 1990).

With respect to the scales' kurtosis, the data in Table 4-3 indicate, as was the case for the MMPI-2, that the uniform transformation, in and of itself, does not have a great effect on the range of kurtosis, which, in turn, does not have a significant impact on percentile equivalence. However, the negative kurtosis (indicating a relatively flat top to the distribution) of most of the MMPI-A Content Scales is transformed into a positive kurtosis (indicating a relatively peaked distribution), which characterizes the MMPI-2 uniform distribution. Although, as just indicated, differential kurtosis is not closely linked to differential

TABLE 4-3. Effects of uniform T-score transformation on skewness and kurtosis in the normative sample

	Skewness				Kurtosis			
	Boys		Girls		Boys		Girls	
Scale	Lin	Uni	Lin	Uni	Lin	Uni	Lin	Uni
A-anx	.284	.695	.106	.793	−.380	.379	−.777	.421
A-obs	.075	.777	−.077	.731	−.635	.313	−.740	.289
A-dep	.590	.711	.422	.756	.047	.702	−.337	.542
A-hea	.748	.783	.688	.715	−.309	.549	.064	.569
A-biz	.667	.755	.722	.743	−.172	.526	.032	.608
A-ang	.040	.796	−.014	.774	−.603	.514	−.587	.264
A-cyn	−.219	.771	−.276	.733	−.730	.149	−.708	.117
A-aln	.327	.798	.467	.706	−.343	.925	−.361	.554
A-con	.168	.774	.277	.710	−.421	.616	−.422	.712
A-lse	.350	.687	.393	.724	−.470	.430	−.280	.633
A-las	.028	.804	.136	.825	−.634	.724	−.354	.656
A-sod	.242	.649	.486	.784	−.224	.661	−.221	.680
A-fam	.172	.718	.085	.763	−.664	.478	−.683	.494
A-sch	.225	.787	.444	.714	−.662	.567	−.228	.636
A-trt	.153	.861	.075	.763	−.585	.946	−.608	.658
M	.257	.758	.262	.749	−.452	.565	−.414	.522
SD	.256	.055	.286	.035	.222	.212	.266	.175
Range	.967	.174	.998	.119	.777	.797	.841	.563

Note: Lin refers to linear T scores and Uni to uniform T scores; n = 805 boys, 815 girls.

percentile values, the imposition of a positive kurtosis would make the comparison of adult and adolescent samples more accurate because they would be based on similarly shaped distributions of scores when comparisons are based on uniform T scores.

The effect of the uniform transformation is seen most directly when percentile levels for equal T scores are compared. These data are presented in Table 4-4, which includes percentiles corresponding to T scores of 70 and 80 in the MMPI-A normative sample. Thus, for example, the percentile corresponding to a linear T score of 70 for boys on A-hea is 96.2, whereas for the same linear T score on A-las, the percentile is 99.3. In contrast, the range of percentiles for uniform T scores of 70 is 96.2-97.3. The mean percentiles for boys and girls at uniform T score 70 (96.8 and 96.6, respectively) are almost identical to the comparable means on the MMPI-2 (96.5 and 96.4, respectively), further illustrating the success of achieving percentile equivalence across the two forms.

The percentile figures at the T score 80 level illustrate yet another effect of using the adult composite distribution in standardizing MMPI-A scores. Where no percentile is reported for a scale (Table

TABLE 4-4. Linear versus uniform T-score percentiles at T scores 70 and 80 in the normative sample

| | Percentiles at T score 70 | | | | Percentiles at T score 80 | | | |
| | Boys | | Girls | | Boys | | Girls | |
Scale	Lin	Uni	Lin	Uni	Lin	Uni	Lin	Uni
A-anx	97.4	96.7	99.4	96.3	100.0	99.6	—	99.7
A-obs	99.0	97.0	99.3	97.5	—	99.8	—	99.0
A-dep	97.1	96.9	97.2	96.3	99.7	99.5	—	99.4
A-hea	96.2	96.2	96.4	96.4	100.0	99.8	99.4	99.4
A-biz	97.2	96.8	96.6	96.4	99.9	99.8	99.8	99.8
A-ang	99.3	97.0	99.1	96.8	—	99.8	—	99.7
A-cyn	99.9	96.5	100.0	96.5	—	99.9	—	99.9
A-aln	98.1	97.3	97.5	97.0	99.8	99.5	99.9	99.5
A-con	98.5	97.0	98.4	97.1	99.9	99.4	99.9	99.4
A-lse	97.7	96.7	97.5	96.8	—	99.9	99.9	99.5
A-las	99.3	97.3	98.6	96.7	—	99.5	—	99.6
A-sod	97.4	96.9	97.5	96.3	99.8	99.3	99.6	99.5
A-fam	98.3	96.4	98.7	96.2	—	99.3	—	99.7
A-sch	98.5	96.5	97.5	96.8	—	99.7	99.9	99.6
A-trt	98.8	96.9	98.9	96.6	99.9	99.5	—	99.4
M	98.2	96.8	98.2	96.6	99.9	99.6	99.8	99.6
SD	1.0	0.31	1.08	0.36	0.1	0.21	0.2	0.16
Range	3.7	1.1	3.6	1.3	0.3	0.6	0.5	0.5

Note: Lin refers to linear T scores and Uni to uniform T scores; n = 805 boys, 815 girls.

4-4), no subject in the normative sample scored as high as linear T score 80. By calibrating the MMPI-A Content Scales to the more highly skewed adult uniform distribution, we are able to stretch the adolescent T scores a little further than we could had we developed a new composite based on the adolescent normative sample. The apparent lack of improvement in terms of percentile equivalence at T score 80 is an artifact of the ceiling effect just noted.

Sample Means and Standard Deviations

Tables 4-5 and 4-6 provide raw score and uniform T-score means and standard deviations for boys and girls in the normative and clinical samples, respectively. Of note in these tables is the relative lack of elevation of scores on the MMPI-A Content Scales in the clinical sample, a problem that has plagued MMPI interpretations for adolescents (see Chapter 1). This pattern is similar to the one found for the MMPI-A clinical scales in the two samples (Butcher et al., 1992). Several fac-

TABLE 4-5. Raw and uniform T-score means and standard deviations in the normative sample

	Raw scores				Uniform T scores			
	Boys		Girls		Boys		Girls	
Scale	M	SD	M	SD	M	SD	M	SD
A-anx	7.8	4.1	9.0	4.4	49.9	10.0	50.1	10.1
A-obs	6.9	3.3	7.9	3.2	49.9	9.9	49.8	9.9
A-dep	7.6	4.6	9.2	5.1	50.0	9.9	50.0	9.9
A-hea	7.9	5.3	9.0	5.5	50.0	9.8	50.1	9.9
A-biz	4.0	3.1	4.1	3.1	50.0	10.0	50.1	9.7
A-ang	7.9	3.2	8.5	3.1	50.0	9.9	49.8	10.1
A-cyn	12.4	4.5	12.3	4.7	49.8	10.1	50.0	10.0
A-aln	6.0	3.4	5.6	3.5	50.0	9.9	49.9	10.0
A-con	9.6	4.0	8.2	3.9	49.9	10.0	50.1	10.0
A-lse	5.0	3.2	5.8	3.5	50.0	9.9	50.0	9.9
A-las	5.9	2.6	6.0	2.7	50.0	9.9	49.9	10.0
A-sod	8.3	4.4	7.2	4.3	50.2	9.8	49.8	10.0
A-fam	11.4	5.6	12.5	5.7	50.1	9.9	49.9	10.0
A-sch	6.3	3.4	5.8	3.2	50.1	9.9	50.1	9.9
A-trt	9.1	4.2	9.3	4.4	50.0	10.0	50.1	10.0

Note: n = 805 boys, 815 girls.

tors may play a role in producing this effect. First, the heterogeneous nature of the clinical sample may lead to a "canceling out" effect that would not be present were the sample divided into more homogeneous subsamples. Second, although most of the subjects in the clinical sample were hospitalized, their problems tended to be concentrated in the realm of alcohol and drug problems and conduct disorders, while there were far fewer cases of mood or psychotic disorders. Third, it is possible that adolescents, as a group, do not manifest the full spectrum of psychopathology that adults exhibit. Finally, we have already noted that the assessment of psychopathology in adolescents is less precise than for adults. Further research will be necessary to identify how (and how much) each of these factors contributes to the low scale elevations among clinical subjects. From a clinical standpoint, the case illustrations provided in Chapter 6 demonstrate that it is possible to find considerable elevation in the MMPI-A profiles of individual adolescents.

These data illustrate the considerations described previously with respect to drawing the "black line" on the MMPI-A profile sheet. Since in both the standard scales and MMPI-A Content Scales, elevations in the clinical sample appeared to be somewhat lower than in adult clinical samples scored on the MMPI-2 norms, it was decided that the area

TABLE 4-6. Raw and uniform T-score means and standard deviations in the clinical sample

	Raw scores				Uniform T scores			
	Boys		Girls		Boys		Girls	
Scale	M	SD	M	SD	M	SD	M	SD
A-anx	8.2	4.3	10.0	5.1	50.9	10.7	52.9	12.4
A-obs	7.0	3.4	7.9	3.6	50.2	10.2	50.4	11.3
A-dep	8.9	5.1	11.6	6.1	52.9	11.2	54.9	12.4
A-hea	6.6	4.6	8.5	5.9	47.5	8.6	49.0	10.7
A-biz	3.6	2.9	3.6	3.1	48.8	9.4	48.8	9.8
A-ang	9.5	3.6	9.4	3.8	55.5	12.9	53.6	13.4
A-cyn	13.0	4.4	12.6	4.9	51.3	10.5	50.8	10.8
A-aln	6.1	3.4	5.9	3.5	50.5	10.2	50.8	10.0
A-con	12.0	4.2	9.8	4.5	56.2	11.8	54.7	12.7
A-lse	5.1	3.2	6.6	3.9	50.3	10.1	52.3	11.4
A-las	6.5	2.9	7.0	2.9	52.8	12.0	53.9	11.9
A-sod	6.8	4.2	6.8	4.9	46.8	9.3	49.2	11.5
A-fam	15.3	5.8	16.8	5.7	57.4	12.1	58.3	12.2
A-sch	9.1	3.5	8.3	3.8	59.0	12.4	58.0	12.8
A-trt	9.0	4.6	9.5	4.7	50.0	11.1	51.0	11.1

Note: $n = 420$ boys, 293 girls.

between T scores 60 and 64 would be shaded to alert clinicians to the possibility of clinically meaningful elevation occurring within this range.

MMPI-A Content Scale Correlations

Final indications of the psychometric functioning of the MMPI-A Content Scales are their intercorrelations and their correlations with the standard scales and Wiggins Content Scales. Tables 4-7 and 4-8 provide the content scale intercorrelations for boys and girls in the normative and clinical samples, respectively. For both genders and both samples, the two scales with the greatest level of correlation with other MMPI-A Content Scales were A-anx and A-trt. Item overlap (see Table 3-3 in Chapter 3) may account for the generally higher level of intercorrelations for the A-trt Scale. This is less likely for the A-anx Scale, as only two of its items are scored on other content scales (A-obs and A-lse). The two scales with the lowest level of correlation are A-cyn and A-las. In general, the intercorrelations among the MMPI-A Content Scales are lower than those found among the MMPI-2 Content Scales (Butcher et al., 1990). However, at least in part, this may simply

TABLE 4-7. MMPI-A Content Scales intercorrelations in the normative sample

	A-anx	A-obs	A-dep	A-hea	A-biz	A-ang	A-cyn	A-aln	A-con	A-lse	A-las	A-sod	A-fam	A-sch	A-trt
A-anx	—	66	73	50	54	50	43	62	36	60	36	43	53	46	60
A-obs	69	—	55	27	45	52	57	46	44	55	22	26	43	40	58
A-dep	74	61	—	48	56	41	37	69	40	68	39	47	59	53	64
A-hea	56	42	53	—	53	23	07	47	22	47	39	35	48	48	42
A-biz	56	51	56	56	—	36	37	55	41	53	32	33	51	50	56
A-ang	51	54	43	33	44	—	51	38	50	36	16	14	44	40	43
A-cyn	54	60	50	34	49	52	—	42	47	35	10	14	35	31	49
A-aln	61	48	70	50	53	40	54	—	38	62	39	55	61	53	67
A-con	41	44	47	37	52	54	52	50	—	37	30	03	50	56	48
A-lse	62	57	74	46	48	38	45	63	45	—	45	49	51	52	67
A-las	32	31	42	26	24	27	22	37	37	49	—	33	41	48	48
A-sod	31	24	42	29	26	15	23	54	17	48	31	—	28	29	45
A-fam	53	44	57	41	45	47	46	61	53	48	35	28	—	60	56
A-sch	41	39	50	45	44	43	40	52	58	51	53	30	52	—	58
A-trt	62	64	71	48	53	49	61	74	56	69	48	47	58	57	—

Note: Decimal points have been omitted. Correlations for boys (n = 805) appear above the diagonal; for girls (n = 815), below the diagonal.

TABLE 4-8. MMPI-A Content Scales intercorrelations in the clinical sample

	A-anx	A-obs	A-dep	A-hea	A-biz	A-ang	A-cyn	A-aln	A-con	A-lse	A-las	A-sod	A-fam	A-sch	A-trt
A-anx	—	76	74	60	53	59	46	50	51	67	30	33	43	44	62
A-obs	76	—	68	50	55	59	55	51	51	66	29	37	43	44	62
A-dep	85	72	—	52	48	47	42	62	42	75	39	41	43	44	66
A-hea	62	55	57	—	59	32	28	43	30	47	19	36	25	33	42
A-biz	55	56	48	59	—	35	48	52	39	47	18	29	32	29	52
A-ang	51	52	54	39	45	—	49	40	62	46	29	14	49	46	51
A-cyn	50	59	50	43	51	56	—	49	56	43	18	24	38	35	54
A-aln	62	55	67	48	49	47	54	—	42	64	40	49	52	37	68
A-con	41	43	39	30	45	62	58	36	—	41	36	10	48	59	57
A-lse	76	69	79	50	46	43	44	59	35	—	46	48	43	44	71
A-las	41	35	52	23	23	39	28	37	32	48	—	27	36	53	47
A-sod	47	42	40	32	31	13	26	57	03	48	22	—	09	19	39
A-fam	39	30	39	34	35	39	39	50	41	29	29	13	—	46	51
A-sch	46	42	51	33	34	47	44	44	54	45	54	21	42	—	51
A-trt	67	64	73	48	47	56	55	71	49	69	49	44	37	52	—

Note: Decimal points have been omitted. Correlations for boys (n = 420) appear above the diagonal; for girls (n = 293), below the diagonal.

be a function of the adolescents scales' somewhat lower level of reliability. Once more, this is an empirical question that should be addressed in future research.

Correlations between the MMPI-A basic and content scales are presented in Tables 4-9 through 4-12. Overall, these data illustrate con-

TABLE 4-9. MMPI-A Content Scales correlations with basic scales in the boys normative sample

	A-anx	A-obs	A-dep	A-hea	A-biz	A-ang	A-cyn	A-aln	A-con	A-lse	A-las	A-sod	A-fam	A-sch	A-trt
L	15	35	08	28	06	33	39	02	29	02	12	14	01	02	06
F1	39	21	52	63	64	25	11	55	39	47	42	34	59	64	50
F2	42	26	53	61	68	24	14	56	35	55	45	40	56	60	58
F	43	25	55	65	70	26	13	59	38	54	46	40	61	65	58
K	56	66	44	06	33	61	72	40	37	39	07	22	33	26	44
Hs	54	27	50	90	47	23	09	46	18	44	37	35	45	40	37
D	50	14	54	55	27	02	10	43	05	45	36	46	29	24	29
Hy	21	15	26	63	16	14	39	15	09	12	24	11	20	15	01
Pd	54	33	64	49	46	33	23	57	43	42	38	21	67	51	43
Mf	27	14	20	11	04	00	13	11	14	16	02	20	09	11	01
Pa	53	34	62	58	64	24	05	56	25	47	35	35	50	44	45
Pt	83	76	79	48	60	54	50	64	43	69	38	46	56	52	63
Sc	74	58	79	64	77	49	43	73	50	66	46	47	72	63	69
Ma	37	50	32	18	44	50	54	29	59	25	09	07	46	38	37
Si	54	40	56	39	34	21	23	58	07	61	43	81	36	32	52

Note: Decimal points have been omitted. Underlining denotes a negative correlation. $n = 805$.

TABLE 4-10. MMPI-A Content Scales correlations with basic scales in the girls normative sample

	A-anx	A-obs	A-dep	A-hea	A-biz	A-ang	A-cyn	A-aln	A-con	A-lse	A-las	A-sod	A-fam	A-sch	A-trt
L	19	30	14	06	02	31	19	01	25	12	10	14	11	10	08
F1	36	27	50	54	60	29	30	59	54	47	37	35	55	61	54
F2	41	32	54	55	63	34	31	60	49	54	38	46	51	56	60
F	42	32	55	58	65	34	32	64	54	54	40	44	56	61	61
K	62	68	53	31	41	62	70	50	40	48	23	29	46	35	55
Hs	62	44	59	91	50	33	36	48	33	49	29	29	40	42	46
D	60	33	68	51	34	13	22	53	17	57	35	47	37	31	47
Hy	33	03	34	56	20	03	12	15	03	19	14	02	17	16	08
Pd	59	41	68	49	51	39	40	59	50	49	31	19	68	46	51
Mf	07	05	04	13	20	07	16	11	28	06	10	06	09	21	16
Pa	56	41	63	54	60	28	15	55	38	49	23	27	42	38	47
Pt	84	78	81	58	62	58	57	63	49	73	42	39	53	50	69
Sc	76	67	79	68	78	54	56	71	60	69	44	41	66	56	74
Ma	43	48	36	36	52	46	51	33	57	26	11	11	47	36	36
Si	49	43	55	34	28	25	36	57	19	65	47	79	34	36	58

Note: Decimal points have been omitted. Underlining denotes a negative correlation. $n = 815$.

siderable independence between the clinical scales and MMPI-A Content Scales, although correlations between certain scales assessing the same domain (e.g., Scale 1 and A-hea) are quite high. These correla-

TABLE 4-11. MMPI-A Content Scales correlations with basic scales in the boys clinical sample

	A-anx	A-obs	A-dep	A-hea	A-biz	A-ang	A-cyn	A-aln	A-con	A-lse	A-las	A-sod	A-fam	A-sch	A-trt
L	41	42	33	13	17	47	33	16	43	27	24	03	35	30	25
F1	41	40	46	47	53	39	37	56	46	46	37	28	54	56	56
F2	53	47	57	62	65	35	37	62	38	60	36	45	38	40	67
F	53	49	58	61	66	41	41	66	46	59	40	41	50	52	69
K	67	71	56	40	49	65	71	55	54	58	27	35	44	41	57
Hs	62	50	57	90	55	30	25	41	32	50	24	35	27	37	42
D	47	30	60	44	20	08	03	30	03	44	23	42	12	24	26
Hy	18	01	26	43	11	13	36	02	11	07	11	00	05	10	03
Pd	46	40	58	26	33	39	29	42	39	36	35	04	59	45	39
Mf	25	21	23	11	07	03	11	12	15	19	09	22	18	03	06
Pa	60	51	60	52	58	40	19	52	31	47	18	29	37	28	46
Pt	86	82	81	62	58	58	51	58	52	73	38	45	43	49	65
Sc	77	74	76	71	74	55	56	69	56	71	40	43	56	49	71
Ma	43	50	32	33	45	45	56	32	59	26	14	04	43	34	39
Si	52	51	56	40	29	31	33	54	21	65	42	81	23	31	51

Note: Decimal points have been omitted. Underlining denotes a negative correlation. $n = 420$.

TABLE 4-12. MMPI-A Content Scales correlations with basic scales in the girls clinical sample

	A-anx	A-obs	A-dep	A-hea	A-biz	A-ang	A-cyn	A-aln	A-con	A-lse	A-las	A-sod	A-fam	A-sch	A-trt
L	28	34	29	13	14	35	21	06	40	26	26	02	21	28	26
F1	55	47	55	52	61	44	45	57	51	47	38	26	58	52	53
F2	63	58	66	59	66	48	52	64	43	61	36	41	39	40	62
F	66	58	68	62	70	51	54	68	52	61	41	38	53	51	65
K	67	74	62	51	58	66	76	60	55	59	31	39	39	48	60
Hs	67	57	63	93	56	39	41	50	30	55	27	36	32	36	51
D	65	46	65	51	22	13	13	43	02	61	31	51	11	24	45
Hy	36	13	38	57	18	00	13	13	06	24	18	01	16	14	16
Pd	63	38	60	36	31	41	33	53	43	38	38	12	60	49	49
Mf	03	02	06	07	21	21	31	19	37	09	01	08	08	18	13
Pa	68	55	69	57	61	42	32	65	37	58	37	37	41	32	56
Pt	89	84	87	65	62	55	56	63	47	80	50	50	35	52	70
Sc	80	73	80	71	77	59	61	71	54	70	45	45	51	51	71
Ma	35	45	31	30	50	55	59	27	64	22	15	12	42	36	34
Si	66	56	63	45	34	27	35	59	13	72	42	84	18	32	58

Note: Decimal points have been omitted. Underlining denotes a negative correlation. $n = 293$.

tions range from .00 to .93 in the case of the two scales just mentioned. Obviously, these correlations reflect, in part, item overlap between certain clinical and content scales. Once more, it appears that the

MMPI-A Content Scales A-cyn and A-las share the least variance with the clinical scales. When examined on a scale-by-scale level, these correlations may provide information pertaining to the internal validity of the MMPI-A Content Scales as reflected by the patterns of their correlations with the standard scales. Following are observations concerning those patterns of correlations that were found to generalize across gender and samples.

A-anx is most highly related with markers of the first factor of the MMPI (e.g., Scales 7 and 8) and less highly related with markers of the second factor (e.g., Scales L, K, 2, 3, and 9), and the third and fourth factors (Scales 5 and 0, respectively). This pattern supports the interpretation of A-anx as a measure of general maladjustment. The pattern of correlations for A-obs is, in general, similar to the one found for A-anx, the noted exception being a lesser tendency for covariation with Scale 8, indicating that elevation on this scale might be reflective of more specified (as opposed to generalized) maladjustment manifesting in obsessive-compulsive tendencies. Scores on A-dep are more highly related with Scale 2 than are those for the previous two content scales, supporting the interpretation of depressive symptomatology for elevations on this scale. In addition, there are indications that, like A-anx, this scale may be a marker of the MMPI general maladjustment factor.

As has already been noted, correlations between A-hea and the standard scales illustrate quite clearly that this content scale measures attributes quite similar to those indexed by Scale 1. Interestingly, correlations between A-hea and Scale 3 are of a moderate level, as is the case for the adult MMPI-2 HEA scale. The pattern of correlations for A-biz support its interpretation as a measure of thought dysfunction, given that, among the standard scales, it is most highly associated with Scale 8.

Interestingly, across gender and samples the highest (in absolute value) correlating standard scale for A-ang was K. Since the function of K as a validity indicator for adolescents is uncertain (hence the decision not to adopt the K correction for the MMPI-A), the meaning of this correlation may be more closely tied to personality characteristics associated with Scale K. This suggests the possibility that adolescents who score high on A-ang may be experiencing considerable turmoil and a general reduction in their psychological defenses, which is manifested symptomatically in outbursts of anger. The pattern of standard scale correlations for A-cyn is rather similar to that of A-ang, the primary difference being a general trend toward lower correlations with Scale 4 and higher correlations with Scale 0, suggesting that high scorers on A-cyn would be less likely to act out their frustrations than those who score high on A-ang, and that their reaction to situational stress may be manifested more strongly in their attitudes than in their behavior.

Standard scale correlations with A-aln are somewhat difficult to interpret because the three standard scales (4, 8, and 0) with which scores on A-aln are most highly correlated are all known to contain items pertaining to alienation. Thus, it is likely that these correlations reflect the alienation-related content of the standard scales rather than the specific symptomatic features of these rather disparate standard scales. Correlations between A-con and the standard scales (particularly Scales 4, 8, and 9) support its interpretation as a measure of disturbed, overactive, acting-out behaviors.

The standard scales associated with A-lse (7, 8, 0) suggest that elevations on this scale may be found in adolescents who display a combination of high anxiety and social introversion coupled with tendencies toward feeling alienated from family and perhaps also from peers. As already indicated, scores on the A-las Scale generally appear to be less highly related to scores on the standard scales, supporting the notion that this scale taps variance pertaining to achievement orientation (or lack thereof) not previously accessible with the MMPI. The high correlation between A-sod and Scale 0 supports the interpretation of the former as a measure of general social introversion.

Correlations between A-fam and Scales 4 and 8 likely reflect the familial discord components that have been identified in the two clinical scales. As is the case for the A-las Scale, correlations between A-sch and the standard scales are generally lower than for other MMPI-A Content Scales, suggesting that elevations on A-sch are indicative of maladaptive behavior that is not readily tapped by the standard scales. Thus, the validation of this scale will be more appropriately based on external rather than internal correlates. Correlations between A-trt and the standard scales also tend to be relatively low in magnitude.

Overall, the correlations presented in Tables 4-9 through 4-12 indicate that some MMPI-A Content Scales measure constructs and attributes not assessed by the clinical scales, whereas other MMPI-A Content Scales share a considerable proportion of variance (and, at times, items) with the standard scales. Further research on the incremental validity of the MMPI-A Content Scales (in reference to the standard scales) is currently under way. Initial findings presented by Ben-Porath and Williams (1991) demonstrate that the MMPI-A Content Scales have considerable incremental validity with respect to the task of differential diagnosis of psychopathology in adolescents.

Finally, Tables 4-13 through 4-16 present correlations between the MMPI-A Content Scales and the Wiggins Content Scales. In general, scales measuring the same constructs on the two sets of scales are quite highly correlated. Interestingly, the three MMPI-A Content Scales de-

TABLE 4-13. Correlations between the MMPI-A Content Scales and Wiggins Content Scales for the boys normative sample

	HEA	DEP	ORG	FAM	AUT	FEM	REL	HOS	MOR	PHO	PSY	HYP	SOC
A-anx	48	81	53	51	35	16	00	44	75	45	65	36	38
A-obs	23	67	30	42	47	09	09	56	73	38	59	55	27
A-dep	43	88	53	53	32	17	−09	39	73	43	63	25	40
A-hea	82	51	89	38	07	20	−11	15	36	54	51	−02	26
A-biz	47	60	57	41	34	22	−01	37	49	46	88	27	23
A-ang	19	51	26	41	49	−02	07	76	46	22	47	58	10
A-cyn	02	43	10	35	84	−07	05	65	51	10	53	57	13
A-aln	48	67	51	50	35	13	−07	35	61	42	64	19	47
A-con	19	42	28	38	67	−01	−15	55	40	19	47	39	−02
A-lse	42	69	53	41	27	18	−04	33	76	49	57	22	45
A-las	39	45	46	28	13	13	−10	11	35	36	30	−07	30
A-sod	37	48	37	22	03	12	−06	09	41	41	37	−04	87
A-fam	42	61	53	87	37	13	−16	40	49	36	56	22	21
A-sch	44	54	52	46	37	07	−17	36	46	39	54	18	22
A-trt	39	69	46	45	40	10	−02	42	66	47	63	30	39

Note: Decimal points have been omitted. $n = 805$.

TABLE 4-14. Correlations between the MMPI-A Content Scales and Wiggins Content Scales for the girls normative sample

	HEA	DEP	ORG	FAM	AUT	FEM	REL	HOS	MOR	PHO	PSY	HYP	SOC
A-anx	54	82	58	49	46	01	−01	55	75	49	68	42	28
A-obs	39	68	46	41	51	08	05	62	75	46	65	52	25
A-dep	51	91	55	52	45	02	−04	48	77	45	66	25	38
A-hea	78	57	88	34	32	09	01	35	41	42	60	24	21
A-biz	49	59	61	36	46	02	06	49	46	42	88	36	17
A-ang	27	51	39	43	50	01	−01	78	48	36	52	54	07
A-cyn	31	55	37	41	86	01	02	65	56	34	61	50	17
A-aln	44	72	54	50	47	16	−05	45	58	35	63	20	46
A-con	32	50	43	41	68	09	−09	60	40	24	53	36	08
A-lse	43	75	54	39	40	07	−04	43	77	46	57	22	47
A-las	25	46	34	26	24	10	−02	26	40	25	24	03	31
A-sod	28	44	32	21	17	17	−04	20	38	32	32	13	87
A-fam	37	60	45	88	46	13	−03	48	46	29	52	25	19
A-sch	39	54	50	38	46	16	−06	40	43	31	47	23	25
A-trt	43	75	55	48	54	12	−02	55	69	46	63	32	43

Note: Decimal points have been omitted. $n = 815$.

veloped specifically for use with adolescents (i.e., A-aln, A-las, A-sch) are the least correlated with the Wiggins Content Scales, indicating that, as intended when new items were written for the MMPI-A, these new scales tap into domains that are not assessed in the adult form.

TABLE 4-15. Correlations between the MMPI-A Content Scales and Wiggins Content Scales for the boys clinical sample

	HEA	DEP	ORG	FAM	AUT	FEM	REL	HOS	MOR	PHO	PSY	HYP	SOC
A-anx	53	84	61	40	36	17	10	60	80	53	65	56	34
A-obs	40	79	53	41	43	17	12	65	77	51	66	62	37
A-dep	47	89	56	39	28	14	03	50	80	39	59	39	43
A-hea	78	58	86	20	16	20	09	37	48	48	64	33	29
A-biz	46	53	60	29	35	21	11	48	47	45	88	43	21
A-ang	23	56	36	43	44	00	06	79	55	31	47	61	14
A-cyn	19	49	33	35	84	06	08	64	52	27	60	59	20
A-aln	33	61	49	42	36	16	−01	45	55	40	61	35	48
A-con	27	50	38	38	68	−08	−02	69	45	20	46	54	13
A-lse	39	75	54	37	29	17	04	48	79	46	56	41	51
A-las	16	39	33	28	20	12	−15	25	36	16	18	12	31
A-sod	32	44	39	06	08	21	06	16	41	48	37	10	88
A-fam	19	45	32	89	33	03	−03	49	46	15	38	35	12
A-sch	29	47	42	38	42	−05	−10	44	43	23	35	33	24
A-trt	36	68	51	40	44	12	04	56	66	45	62	47	43

Note: Decimal points have been omitted. *n* = 420.

TABLE 4-16. Correlations between the MMPI-A Content Scales and Wiggins Content Scales for the girls clinical sample

	HEA	DEP	ORG	FAM	AUT	FEM	REL	HOS	MOR	PHO	PSY	HYP	SOC
A-anx	60	89	67	36	38	−08	01	53	82	55	72	47	44
A-obs	54	78	56	27	44	−03	04	58	78	50	70	57	40
A-dep	54	94	62	35	35	−11	00	52	84	44	67	40	40
A-hea	81	59	89	29	34	−08	06	43	51	42	64	38	30
A-biz	50	55	67	30	43	−06	−03	54	45	35	87	56	26
A-ang	36	58	44	30	51	−10	−06	82	50	22	55	59	11
A-cyn	43	56	41	31	86	−08	−02	71	51	33	68	60	20
A-aln	48	67	49	40	38	−22	04	48	58	33	66	29	50
A-con	32	44	38	28	70	−13	−09	68	41	20	53	57	01
A-lse	50	79	57	27	32	−12	02	42	85	47	60	36	55
A-las	28	53	31	20	22	−09	−07	33	48	21	31	20	27
A-sod	40	45	34	14	10	−13	02	12	43	40	41	01	91
A-fam	26	40	37	89	33	−11	−03	42	31	12	40	31	11
A-sch	34	52	38	30	47	−16	−10	45	44	18	43	37	22
A-trt	48	73	53	28	44	−18	−06	57	70	40	61	42	42

Note: Decimal points have been omitted. *n* = 293.

Concluding Comments

The data presented and discussed in this chapter demonstrate that the MMPI-A Content Scales possess adequate psychometric strength. Their reliability (in terms of internal consistency and test-retest), though somewhat lower than that of the MMPI-2 Content Scales, is comparable to that of other scales developed for use with adolescents. As indicated above, this reflects the need for interpretive caution, which might best be exercised by using somewhat wider confidence intervals around adolescent scale scores than are typically drawn around adult scale scores. Employing such an extra measure of caution should compensate for the slight attenuation in reliability noted in this chapter.

This chapter also provided a description of the rationale and procedure for developing uniform T scores for the MMPI-A Content Scales, and data illustrating the effects and efficacy of the uniform transformation. These data indicate that the goals of achieving percentile comparability within the MMPI-A scales and in reference to MMPI-2 scales were accomplished.

Finally, correlations between the MMPI-A Content Scales and a variety of other MMPI/MMPI-A scales were presented to provide the reader with an indication of how the MMPI-A Content Scales overlap with other MMPI measures and the extent to which the content scales contribute new information. Overall, we observed less interrelatedness for the MMPI-A Content Scales than had been reported for the MMPI-2 Content Scales. Some new scales such as A-hea were found to correlate very highly with the MMPI-A scales, whereas others, such as A-las, had much lower correlations with other MMPI-A scales. Research with the MMPI-2 Content Scales (Ben-Porath et al., 1991) has demonstrated that even when the content scales correlate rather highly with the MMPI-2 standard scales, they are able to convey incrementally significant information beyond what is obtained from the standard scales. Research with the MMPI-A Content Scales has demonstrated a similar pattern of incremental validity for these scales (Ben-Porath & Williams, 1991).

The data presented in this chapter indicate that the MMPI-A Content Scales are built on a solid psychometric foundation, one that should make them quite useful in the prediction of extratest data. Their success in this realm is illustrated and specific extratest correlates are presented in the following chapter.

Chapter 5

Validity of the MMPI-A
Content Scales

The MMPI-A Content Scales were constructed primarily on the basis of item content. Initially, items were grouped together into scales if they were judged to be assessing similar characteristics. The scales were then refined using internal consistency procedures. Because the resulting scales are quite homogeneous, examination of item content in the scales provides important information about what adolescents are saying about themselves in responding to the MMPI-A items.

In addition, important information about what the scales measure can be obtained by examining relations between content scale scores and other appropriate measures. Data concerning relationships between the MMPI-A Content Scales and other MMPI-A scales (validity and clinical) were reported in Chapter 4. These data offer some evidence of the validity of the content scales. They suggest that some of the scales are measuring characteristics very similar to those measured by other MMPI-A scales. For example, the correlations of .81 (normative boys) and .79 (normative girls) between Scale 0 and the Social Discomfort (A-sod) Scale (see Tables 4-9 and 4-10, in Chapter 4) suggest that both are measuring introversion, shyness, and social discomfort. Other MMPI-A Content Scales seem to have only modest correlations with the instrument's basic scales, suggesting that they assess different characteristics. Although such data offer some insight into the validity of the MMPI-A Content Scales, more definitive validity information is conveyed by relations between MMPI-A Content Scale scores and extratest variables and ratings.

In this chapter we will present data on the extratest correlates of the MMPI-A Content Scales. Such extratest data are available for the MMPI-A normative subjects and for subjects from the several different clinical settings described in Chapter 2. The sources of extratest data include self-reported biographical and stressful life events information, parent ratings, teacher ratings, mental health staff ratings, and information obtained from records of clinical subjects. Detailed

TABLE 5-1. Correlates for the A-anx Scale for normative and clinical boys and girls (14-18 years)

		Normative sample		Clinical sample	
Source	Scale or item	Boys	Girls	Boys	Girls
LE	Increase in disagreements with parent(s)	NS	.19	.20	.27
LE	Parents' arguments worsened	NS	.19	NS	NS
RR	Depression	NA	NA	NS	.23
RR	Somatic complaints	NA	NA	NS	.20

Note: LE refers to Life Events Form, RR to Record Review. All correlations (*r*) are Pearson product-moment correlation coefficients with $p \leq .0005$ and an absolute magnitude $\geq .18$. NS (not significant) indicates the correlate did not reach these significance criteria. NA (not available) indicates that these measures were not collected for the normative subjects.

descriptions of each of these information sources and the procedures used to collect the data are presented in Chapter 2.

The validity analyses described in this chapter were conducted using correlations between MMPI-A Content Scale raw scores and extratest information for both normative and clinical subjects. Because large numbers of correlations were computed for each content scale, familywise error rate was taken into account by considering only correlations that attained an absolute magnitude greater than .18 and were statistically significant beyond the .0005 level. The following is a scale-by-scale description of the results of the validity analyses.

Results of the Validity Analyses

Adolescent Anxiety (A-anx)

Table 5-1 indicates that the Adolescent-Anxiety (A-anx) Scale had few significant correlates for normal subjects (none for boys and two for girls). This probably reflects the absence of appropriate anxiety items in the measures used with the normal boys and girls. For clinical boys, there was only one significant correlate (Table 5-1). Higher scorers indicated they had experienced increases in disagreements with parents. Clinical girls scoring higher on A-anx also reported increases in disagreements with parents (Table 5-1). In addition, these girls were reported to be more depressed and to have more somatic symptoms than lower scorers on this scale.

In summary, our data offered only limited information concerning the validity of the A-anx Scale. It may be measuring general malad-

TABLE 5-2. Correlates for the A-obs Scale for normative and clinical boys and girls (14-18 years)

		Normative sample		Clinical sample	
Source	Scale or item	Boys	Girls	Boys	Girls
LE	Increase in disagreements with parent(s)	NS	.19	NS	.22
DAB	Neurotic/Dependent Behaviors	NA	NA	.19	NS
RR	Suicidal ideations/Gestures	NA	NA	NS	.21

Note: LE refers to Life Events Form, DAB to Devereux Adolescent Behavior Rating Scale, RR to Record Review. All correlations (r) are Pearson product-moment correlation coefficients with $p \leqslant .0005$ and an absolute magnitude $\geqslant .18$. NS (not significant) indicates the correlate did not reach these significance criteria. NA (not available) indicates that these measures were not collected for the normative subjects.

justment as well as specific symptoms such as depression and somatic complaints. More studies are needed to determine if it has additional correlates for normal and clinical subjects.

Obsessiveness (A-obs)

There were only four significant correlates for the Adolescent-Obsessiveness (A-obs) Scale in the four samples studied (Table 5-2). There were no significant correlates for normal boys. Both normal and clinical girls who scored higher on this scale reported increases in disagreements with parents. For clinical boys, higher scores were associated with neurotic/dependent characteristics, such as seeking out help and attention from adults, being obsessed and worried, and blaming themselves for perceived bad behavior. The records of clinical girls who scored higher on the A-obs Scale indicated that they were more likely to have had suicidal ideas and/or to have made suicidal gestures. Although these significant correlates are consistent with the way we have conceptualized the A-obs Scale, there is some concern that the scale was not significantly related to parent ratings of obsessive-compulsive behavior (CBCL) for clinical boys or to parent ratings of anxious-obsessive behavior (CBCL) for clinical girls. Perhaps the professional staff members who completed the DAB were more sensitive to these particular kinds of problems than were the parents who completed the CBCL.

Based on the limited data currently available, it can be concluded that A-obs elevations may be suggestive of some general maladjustment and also of dependent, anxious behaviors for clinical boys and suicidal ideation/gestures for clinical girls. Further research with clin-

TABLE 5-3. Correlates for the A-dep Scale for normative and clinical boys and girls (14-18 years)

Source	Scale or item	Normative sample		Clinical sample	
		Boys	Girls	Boys	Girls
BIO	Marks in school	NS	−.18	NS	NS
LE	Gained much weight	NS	.20	NS	NS
LE	Outstanding personal achievement	NS	−.18	NS	NS
LE	Increase in disagreements with parent(s)	NS	NS	NS	.24
RR	Suicidal ideations/Gestures	NA	NA	.19	.23
RR	History of being sexually abused	NA	NA	.18	NS
RR	Depression	NA	NA	NS	.22
RR	Low self-esteem	NA	NA	NS	.21

Note: BIO refers to Biographical Information Form, LE to Life Events Form, RR to Record Review. All correlations (r) are Pearson product-moment correlation coefficients with $p \leqslant .0005$ and an absolute magnitude $\geqslant .18$. NS (not significant) indicates the correlate did not reach these significance criteria. NA (not available) indicates that these measures were not collected for the normative subjects.

ical subjects known to be exhibiting obsessive symptoms is needed to clarify the interpretation of this scale.

Adolescent Depression (A-dep)

The A-dep Scale had significant correlates for three of the four samples studied (Table 5-3). Only for normal boys were significant correlates not identified. Most of the correlates are consistent with the conceptualization of this scale as a measure of dysphoria/depression. Normal girls who scored higher on the scale had gained much weight, were less likely to have outstanding personal achievement in school, and had poorer marks in school. For both clinical boys and girls, elevations on this scale were associated with suicidal ideation/gestures. In addition, clinical girls scoring higher on this scale were depressed and had low self-esteem. These girls also reported increases in disagreements with parents. Interestingly, for higher-scoring clinical boys, treatment records indicated a history of being sexually abused. Clearly, for normal girls and for clinical boys and girls, elevations on the A-dep Scale are suggestive of behaviors and symptoms of dysphoria/depression, and for clinical subjects suicidal ideas and/or gestures.

TABLE 5-4. Correlates for the A-hea Scale for normative and clinical boys and girls (14-18 years)

Source	Scale or item	Normative sample		Clinical sample	
		Boys	Girls	Boys	Girls
BIO	Number of school problems	.24	.23	NS	NS
BIO	Marks in school	−.22	−.24	NS	NS
BIO	Course failure in school	NS	.20	NS	NS
LE	Repeated grade in school	.21	NS	NS	NS
LE	Suspended from school	.19	.21	NS	NS
LE	Lost much weight	NS	NS	.18	NS
LE	Increase in disagreements with				
	parent(s)	NS	NS	NS	.21
CBCL	Somatic Complaints	NA	NA	.32	.29
CBCL	Schizoid	NA	NA	.26	NS
CBCL	Internalizing	NA	NA	.24	NS
CBCL	Total Behavior Problems	NA	NA	.20	NS
RR	Intellectual level	NA	NA	−.18	NS
RR	Somatic complaints	NA	NA	NS	.27

Note: BIO refers to Biographical Information Form, LE to Life Events Form, CBCL to Child Behavior Checklist, RR to Record Review. All correlations (r) are Pearson product-moment correlation coefficients with $p \leq .0005$ and an absolute magnitude $\geq .18$. NS (not significant) indicates the correlate did not reach these significance criteria. NA (not available) indicates that these measures were not collected for the normative subjects.

Adolescent Health Concerns (A-hea)

Significant correlates were identified for the Health Concerns (A-hea) Scale for all four samples studied (Table 5-4). For both normal boys and girls, higher A-hea scores were associated with poor school performance, suspensions from school, and other school problems. Health concerns and/or somatic symptoms were not identified as correlates because such items were not present in the instruments available for most normal subjects.

For clinical boys and girls, elevations on the A-hea Scale were associated with somatic complaints. That this relationship replicated across genders and across data sources increases our confidence in this correlate. Clinical boys scoring higher on this scale also were rated by parents as having more behavior problems, and the boys' records suggested that higher scorers on this scale tended to be less intellectually capable than lower scorers. The higher-scoring clinical boys also were rated by parents as more schizoid (e.g., guilty, fearful, clinging, worrying, hearing things) and internalizing, and the boys reported having lost much weight recently. For clinical girls, higher scores were associated with increases in disagreements with parents.

In summary, our data offer considerable support for the A-hea

TABLE 5-5. Correlates for the A-biz Scale for normative and clinical boys and girls (14-18 years)

Source	Scale or item	Normative sample		Clinical sample	
		Boys	Girls	Boys	Girls
BIO	Number of school problems	.18	.25	NS	NS
BIO	Marks in school	−.21	−.20	NS	NS
BIO	Course failure in school	NS	.20	NS	NS
BIO	Suspension from school	NS	.18	NS	NS
LE	Arrest of mother or father	NS	NS	NS	.23
LE	Arrest of sister or brother	NS	NS	NS	.22
LE	Increase in disagreements with parent(s)	NS	NS	NS	.20
DAB	Psychotic Behaviors	NA	NA	.21	NS
RR	Record of a child protection worker being assigned in past	NA	NA	.19	NS
RR	Bizarre sensory experiences	NA	NA	NS	.21

Note: BIO refers to Biographical Information Form, LE to Life Events Form, DAB to Devereux Adolescent Behavior Rating Scale, RR to Record Review. All correlations (r) are Pearson product-moment correlation coefficients with $p \leqslant .0005$ and an absolute magnitude $\geqslant .18$. NS (not significant) indicates the correlate did not reach these significance criteria. NA (not available) indicates that these measures were not collected for the normative subjects.

Scale as a measure of somatic complaints in clinical subjects. For normal boys and girls, higher scores on the scale seem to be related to misbehavior, poor academic performance, and other problems in school.

Adolescent Bizarre Mentation (A-biz)

Significant correlates were identified for the Bizarre Mentation (A-biz) Scale for normal and clinical subjects (Table 5-5). For the normal boys and girls, the scale seemed to be measuring general maladjustment. Both normal boys and girls scoring higher on this scale reported having school problems and receiving lower marks in school. In addition, higher-scoring normal girls were more likely to have reported being suspended from school.

In the clinical samples, the A-biz Scale was related to general disruption in the home as well as to symptoms indicative of psychosis. Records of higher-scoring clinical boys were more likely to indicate that a child protection worker had been assigned to the home. Higher-scoring clinical girls were more likely to report arrests of a parent or sibling and increased disagreements with parents. Clinical boys who scored higher on this scale were more likely to have been rated as dis-

TABLE 5-6. Correlates for the A-ang Scale for normative and clinical boys and girls (14-18 years)

		Normative sample		Clinical sample	
Source	Scale or item	Boys	Girls	Boys	Girls
BIO	Number of school problems	NS	.18	.24	.25
BIO	Disciplinary/probation problems in school	NS	NS	.24	NS
BIO	Course failure in school	NS	NS	.21	.26
LE	Increase in disagreements with parent(s)	NS	.19	.21	.22
LE	Change in schools	NS	NS	NS	.22
LE	Court appearance	NS	NS	NS	.19
CBCL	Externalizing	NA	NA	.20	.28
CBCL	Delinquent	NA	NA	NS	.28
CBCL	Aggressive	NA	NA	NS	.26
DAB	Neurotic/Dependent Behaviors	NA	NA	.22	NS
DAB	Acting Out Behaviors	NA	NA	.21	.26
DAB	Heterosexual Interests	NA	NA	NS	.22
RR	History of assaultive behavior	NA	NA	.20	.20
RR	History of being sexually abused	NA	NA	.18	NS
RR	Court involvement for status offense(s)	NA	NA	NS	.21

Note: BIO refers to Biographical Information Form, LE to Life Events Form, CBCL to Child Behavior Checklist, DAB to Devereux Adolescent Behavior Rating Scale, RR to Record Review. All correlations (r) are Pearson product-moment correlation coefficients with $p \leq .0005$ and an absolute magnitude $\geq .18$. NS (not significant) indicates the correlate did not reach these significance criteria. NA (not available) indicates that these measures were not collected for the normative subjects.

playing psychotic behaviors, and the records of clinical girls scoring higher on the scale indicated bizarre sensory experiences.

In summary, our data indicate that the A-biz Scale is a measure of general maladjustment for normal subjects. Higher scorers are likely to have problems in school and to receive low marks. For clinical boys and girls, high scores are suggestive of bizarre sensory experiences and other symptoms and behaviors that may be indicative of psychosis.

Adolescent Anger (A-ang)

The Anger (A-ang) Scale was conceptualized as measuring problems with anger control. There were no significant correlates for the normal boys and two for the normal girls (Table 5-6). Normal girls scoring higher on this scale were more likely to report school problems and increased disagreements with parents. The usefulness of the scale with normal subjects remains to be determined.

There were numerous significant correlates for the A-ang Scale for clinical boys and girls (Table 5-6). Higher-scoring boys and girls were more likely to report academic and conduct problems at school, and higher-scoring girls were more likely to report changing schools. Higher-scoring clinical boys were more likely to have histories of assaultive behavior and to be rated as engaging in acting-out behaviors. These boys also were rated as passive, dependent, and clinging in relationships with adults and as more likely to have been sexually abused. Higher-scoring clinical girls were rated as aggressive, and records indicated histories of assaultive behavior. The higher-scoring clinical girls also were engaged in more acting-out behaviors and had histories of court involvement. They also were rated as engaging in more heterosexual acting-out behaviors and admitted to having experienced increases in disagreements with parents.

In summary, this scale demonstrated considerable external validity for clinical subjects. Higher scorers had histories of assault and other acting-out behaviors. That the pattern of correlates replicated for boys and girls and existed across various data sources lends support to the scale's sensitivity to problems with anger control.

Adolescent Cynicism (A-cyn)

No significant correlates for the Cynicism (A-cyn) Scale were found for any of the four samples studied. The scale was intended to assess the extent to which adolescents hold misanthropic attitudes. Because the measures used to validate the content scales included few items dealing directly with such attitudes, the lack of significant correlates in our data should not be interpreted as indicating that the scale is not valid. It is interesting, however, to note that higher scorers on this scale were not seen as more angry, aggressive, or acting out.

Adolescent Alienation (A-aln)

The A-aln Scale had few significant correlates in the normal samples (Table 5-7). Boys and girls in the normative samples who scored higher on this scale reported receiving lower marks in school. In addition, higher-scoring girls in the normative sample reported having gained much weight in the past six months. In the clinical samples, the significant correlates were consistent with our conceptualization of the A-aln Scale as a measure of emotional distance from others. Records indicated that higher-scoring clinical girls were more likely to have low

TABLE 5-7. Correlates for the A-aln Scale for normative and clinical boys and girls (14-18 years)

		Normative sample		Clinical sample	
Source	Scale or item	Boys	Girls	Boys	Girls
BIO	Marks in school	.20	−.18	NS	NS
LE	Gained much weight	NS	.24	NS	NS
LE	Used drugs or alcohol	NS	NS	−.18	NS
LE	Increase in disagreements with				
	parent(s)	NS	NS	NS	.22
RR	Low self-esteem	NA	NA	.22	NS
RR	Poor social skills	NA	NA	.18	NS
RR	History of few or no friends	NA	NA	NS	.20

Note: BIO refers to Biographical Information Form, LE to Life Events Form, RR to Record Review. All correlations (*r*) are Pearson product-moment correlation coefficients with $p \leqslant .0005$ and an absolute magnitude $\geqslant .18$. NS (not significant) indicates the correlate did not reach these significance criteria. NA (not available) indicates that these measures were not collected for the normative subjects.

self-esteem and poor social skills, and clinical boys had histories of few or no friends. In addition, higher-scoring clinical boys were less likely to self-report drug or alcohol use. Higher-scoring clinical girls reported increases in disagreements with parents.

In summary, our data offer some support for the A-aln Scale as a measure of feeling emotionally distant from others for both normal and clinical samples. However, the evidence is stronger for the clinical samples than for the normal ones—probably at least in part because there were fewer relevant potential correlates for the normal subjects.

Adolescent Conduct Problems (A-con)

The Conduct Problems (A-con) Scale had numerous correlates for both normal and clinical samples (Table 5-8). For both normal boys and girls, higher scores on this scale were associated with use of drugs and alcohol, problems in school, and low marks in school. In addition, higher-scoring normal girls were more likely to have histories of cheating, lying, and other disciplinary problems in school and to have been suspended from school.

Higher scores on the A-con Scale also were associated with behavioral problems in schools for clinical boys and girls. Higher-scoring clinical girls reported poorer marks in school. Both clinical boys and girls scoring higher on this scale were more likely to have had problems with alcohol or other drugs. Other acting-out behaviors and

TABLE 5-8. Correlates for the A-con Scale for normative and clinical boys and girls (14-18 years)

Source	Scale or item	Normative sample		Clinical sample	
		Boys	Girls	Boys	Girls
BIO	Number of school problems	.23	.29	.28	.29
BIO	Marks in school	−.22	−.25	NS	−.26
BIO	Disciplinary/probation problems in school	NS	.19	.27	.26
BIO	Course failure in school	NS	.18	NS	NS
BIO	Suspension from school	NS	.18	NS	NS
LE	Used drugs or alcohol	.24	.28	NS	.27
LE	Increase in disagreements with parent(s)	NS	.25	NS	.22
LE	Caught cheating or lying in school	NS	.21	NS	NS
LE	Suspended from school	NS	.19	NS	.27
LE	Court appearance	NS	NS	NS	.29
LE	Arrested for stealing	NS	NS	NS	.23
LE	Placed on probation	NS	NS	NS	.20
CBCL	Delinquent	NA	NA	.31	.30
CBCL	Externalizing	NA	NA	.23	NS
CBCL	Social Competence: School	NA	NA	−.23	NS
DAB	Acting Out Behaviors	NA	NA	NS	.29
DAB	Heterosexual Interests	NA	NA	NS	.22
RR	Experience with amphetamines	NA	NA	.25	NS
RR	Court involvement for a violent non-status offense(s)	NA	NA	.23	NS
RR	Record of a child protection worker being assigned at present time	NA	NA	.19	NS
RR	Experience with alcohol	NA	NA	.18	.26
RR	Acting out/Irresponsible behavior	NA	NA	.18	NS
RR	Running away	NA	NA	.18	.25
RR	Truancy/School avoidance	NA	NA	NS	.30
RR	Drug use/Abuse	NA	NA	NS	.27
RR	History of being sexually active	NA	NA	NS	.25
RR	Experience with cannabis	NA	NA	NS	.22
RR	Court involvement for status offense(s)	NA	NA	NS	.22
RR	Experience with hallucinogens	NA	NA	NS	.21
RR	Record of previous substance abuse treatment	NA	NA	NS	.21
RR	Depression	NA	NA	NS	−.20

Note: BIO refers to Biographical Information Form, LE to Life Events Form, CBCL to Child Behavior Checklist, DAB to Devereux Adolescent Behavior Rating Scale, RR to Record Review. All correlations (r) are Pearson product-moment correlation coefficients with $p \leq .0005$ and an absolute magnitude $\geq .18$. NS (not significant) indicates the correlate did not reach these significance criteria. NA (not available) indicates that these measures were not collected for the normative subjects.

TABLE 5-9. Correlates for the A-Ise Scale for normative and clinical boys and girls (14-18 years)

		Normative sample		Clinical sample	
Source	Scale or item	Boys	Girls	Boys	Girls
BIO	Marks in school	NS	−.18	NS	NS
LE	Gained much weight	NS	.18	NS	NS
LE	Outstanding personal achievement	NS	−.23	NS	NS
LE	Increase in disagreements with parent(s)	NS	NS	NS	.21
RR	Low self-esteem	NA	NA	.24	.25
RR	History of being sexually abused	NA	NA	.19	NS
RR	Poor social skills	NA	NA	.18	NS
RR	Depression	NA	NA	NS	.26
RR	Suicide ideations/Gestures	NA	NA	NS	.26
RR	History of learning disabilities	NA	NA	NS	.21

Note: BIO refers to Biographical Information Form, LE to Life Events Form, RR to Record Review. All correlations (r) are Pearson product-moment correlation coefficients with $p \leqslant .0005$ and an absolute magnitude $\geqslant .18$. NS (not significant) indicates the correlate did not reach these significance criteria. NA (not available) indicates that these measures were not collected for the normative subjects.

court involvement also were noted for higher scorers. Higher-scoring clinical boys were reported to have run away from home, and higher-scoring girls had histories of being sexually active.

In summary, the A-con Scale was conceptualized as assessing antisocial, acting-out behavior. Our data suggest considerable external validity for this scale. Although there were more correlates for clinical than for normal subjects, higher scores on the scale were associated with behavior problems for all four samples. Not surprisingly, the behavior problems were more numerous and more severe for clinical than for normal subjects. The replication of correlates across gender, samples, and data sources adds confidence to our interpretation of this scale.

Adolescent Low Self-Esteem (A-lse)

The Low Self-Esteem (A-lse) Scale had no significant correlates for normal boys and only three for normal girls (Table 5-9). Normal girls with higher scores described themselves as having gained much weight, as getting poor marks in school, and as not having outstanding personal achievements. Although there were relatively few significant correlates for the clinical subjects, they were quite consistent with our conceptualization of this scale as indicating negative self-opinions.

TABLE 5-10. Correlates for the A-las Scale for normative and clinical boys and girls (14-18 years)

Source	Scale or item	Normative sample		Clinical sample	
		Boys	Girls	Boys	Girls
BIO	Number of school problems	.22	NS	NS	NS
BIO	Marks in school	−.31	−.23	−.31	−.32
BIO	Number of school activities	−.24	−.20	−.25	−.22
LE	Outstanding personal achievement	NS	−.24	NS	NS
LE	Won an outstanding prize or award	NS	NS	NS	−.19
CBCL	Social Competence: Activity	NA	NA	−.21	NS
RR	Running away	NA	NA	.19	NS
RR	Truancy/School avoidance	NA	NA	.18	NS
RR	History of sexual acting out	NA	NA	NS	.20

Note: BIO refers to Biographical Information Form, LE to Life Events Form, CBCL to Child Behavior Checklist, RR to Record Review. All correlations (r) are Pearson product-moment correlation coefficients with $p \leqslant .0005$ and an absolute magnitude $\geqslant .18$. NS (not significant) indicates the correlate did not reach these significance criteria. NA (not available) indicates that these measures were not collected for the normative subjects.

Records of higher-scoring clinical boys and girls indicated that they had low self-esteem. Additionally, there were indications that the clinical boys who scored higher on this scale had poor social skills and histories of having been sexually abused. There were indications of depression and suicidal ideation/gestures in the records of clinical girls who scored higher on this scale. These clinical girls also were more likely to have histories of learning disabilities and to report increased disagreements with parents.

In summary, higher scores on this scale appear to be indicative of adolescents who have negative views of themselves and do poorly in school. For clinical girls, higher scores also seem to be indicative of depression.

Adolescent Low Aspirations (A-las)

We conceptualized high scores on the Low Aspirations (A-las) Scale as indicating disinterest in and low expectations of success. Meaningful correlates for this scale were identified in all four samples studied (Table 5-10). For normal and clinical boys and girls, higher scores were associated with less participation in school activities, poor marks in school, and lack of outstanding performance or achievement. Normal

TABLE 5-11. Correlates for the A-sod Scale for normative and clinical boys and girls (14-18 years)

Source	Scale or item	Normative sample		Clinical sample	
		Boys	Girls	Boys	Girls
BIO	Number of school activities	−.19	NS	NS	NS
LE	Used drugs or alcohol	−.19	NS	NS	−.29
CBCL	Delinquent	NA	NA	NS	−.28
CBCL	Externalizing	NA	NA	NS	−.24
DAB	Withdrawn/Timid Behaviors	NA	NA	NS	.39
DAB	Heterosexual Interests	NA	NA	NS	−.33
DAB	Acting Out Behaviors	NA	NA	NS	−.23
RR	Social withdrawal	NA	NA	.26	.27
RR	History of few or no friends	NA	NA	.19	.25
RR	Depression	NA	NA	NS	.23
RR	Eating problems	NA	NA	NS	.19
RR	Drug use/Abuse	NA	NA	NS	−.31
RR	Acting out/Irresponsible behavior	NA	NA	NS	−.25
RR	History of being sexually active	NA	NA	NS	−.22
RR	Experience with alcohol	NA	NA	NS	−.22
RR	Experience with cannabis	NA	NA	NS	−.22

Note: BIO refers to Biographical Information Form, LE to Life Events Form, CBCL to Child Behavior Checklist, DAB to Devereux Adolescent Behavior Rating Scale, RR to Record Review. All correlations (r) are Pearson product-moment correlation coefficients with $p \leq .0005$ and an absolute magnitude $\geq .18$. NS (not significant) indicates the correlate did not reach these significance criteria. NA (not available) indicates that these measures were not collected for the normative subjects.

boys scoring higher on this scale also reported multiple school problems. Higher-scoring clinical boys had records of running away and truancy. Records of higher-scoring clinical girls indicated that they had histories of sexual acting out.

In summary, the data support the A-las Scale as a measure of poor achievement and limited participation in school activities. In addition, the scale seems to be related to antisocial tendencies such as running away, truancy, and sexual acting out.

Adolescent Social Discomfort (A-sod)

This scale had few significant correlates for normal subjects (two for boys and none for girls) (Table 5-11). Normal boys scoring higher on this scale were less likely to use drugs or alcohol and participated in fewer school activities. There were several significant correlates for clinical boys and many correlates for clinical girls (Table 5-11). Clinical boys and girls were seen as socially withdrawn and as having few or no friends. The clinical girls scoring higher on this scale also were more likely than lower scorers to be depressed and to have eating problems and less likely than lower scorers to be interested in boys, to use drugs or alcohol, or to act out in irresponsible ways.

In summary, the correlates of the A-sod Scale are consistent with our conceptualization of it as a measure of social discomfort and social withdrawal. In addition, for girls the higher scores on the scale may indicate depression or eating problems and contraindicate aggressive and irresponsible acting-out behavior.

Adolescent Family Problems (A-fam)

We identified numerous significant correlates for the Family Problems (A-fam) Scale for normal and clinical boys and girls (Table 5-12). As expected, higher scorers reported increased disagreements with parents and worsening of arguments between parents. They also were more likely to have school problems of various kinds and to show poor academic performance.

For clinical subjects, higher scores on the A-fam Scale were associated with a wide variety of symptoms and problems, and both boys and girls were reported to have been delinquent, hostile, and aggressive. Interestingly, higher scores for clinical subjects also were associated with more neurotic behaviors such as internalizing, dependency, and withdrawal. Clinical boys with higher scores had histories of physical abuse, and clinical girls with higher scores had histories of sexual abuse.

In summary, higher scorers on the A-fam Scale tend to report disagreements with and between parents. Higher scores also are associated with a wide variety of both acting-out and neurotic symptoms and behaviors. It is not possible to determine from our data if adolescents from troubled families develop acting-out and/or neurotic behaviors or if the acting-out and/or neurotic behaviors lead to conflicts with and between parents. Longitudinal research would be necessary to address causality. At any rate, it can be inferred that higher scorers on the A-fam Scale are likely to be experiencing family conflicts and displaying a wide variety of acting-out and/or neurotic behaviors.

Adolescent School Problems (A-sch)

There were many significant correlates of the School Problems (A-sch)

TABLE 5-12. Correlates for the A-fam Scale for normative and clinical boys and girls (14-18 years)

Source	Scale or item	Normative sample		Clinical sample	
		Boys	Girls	Boys	Girls
BIO	Number of school problems	.29	.28	NS	NS
BIO	Marks in school	−.29	−.23	−.18	NS
BIO	Course failure in school	NS	.21	.20	NS
LE	Increase in disagreements with parent(s)	.33	.41	.30	.48
LE	Suspended from school	.20	NS	NS	NS
LE	Parents' arguments worsened	.19	.22	NS	NS
LE	Gained much weight	NS	.19	NS	NS
LE	Lost my job	NS	.18	NS	NS
LE	Failed a major exam or course	NS	.18	NS	NS
CBCL	Delinquent	NA	NA	.32	.42
CBCL	Externalizing	NA	NA	.30	.43
CBCL	Total Behavior Problems	NA	NA	.28	.38
CBCL	Aggressive	NA	NA	.24	.39
CBCL	Hostile/Withdrawal	NA	NA	.22	*
CBCL	Internalizing	NA	NA	.21	.23
CBCL	Uncommunicative	NA	NA	.20	*
CBCL	Social Competence: Activities	NA	NA	−.25	NS
CBCL	Social Competence: School	NA	NA	−.23	NS
CBCL	Cruel	NA	NA	*	.33
CBCL	Depression/Withdrawal	NA	NA	*	.26
CBCL	Immature/Hyperactive	NA	NA	*	.25
DAB	Neurotic/Dependent Behaviors	NA	NA	.20	NS
DAB	Heterosexual Interests	NA	NA	NS	.25
RR	Running away	NA	NA	.26	NS
RR	History of being physically abused	NA	NA	.18	NS
RR	History of being sexually abused	NA	NA	NS	.24

Note: BIO refers to Biographical Information Form, LE to Life Events Form, CBCL to Child Behavior Checklist, DAB to Devereux Adolescent Behavior Rating Scale, RR to Record Review. All correlations (r) are Pearson product-moment correlation coefficients with $p \leqslant .0005$ and an absolute magnitude $\geqslant .18$. NS (not significant) indicates the correlate did not reach these significance criteria. NA (not available) indicates that these measures were not collected for the normative subjects.

*Scale is not scored for this gender (Achenbach & Edelbrock, 1983).

Scale for all four samples studied (Table 5-13). As expected, higher scorers reported numerous school difficulties, including poor academic performance and disciplinary problems of various kinds. Higher-scoring normal boys and girls participated in fewer school activities. Clinical subjects with higher scores had histories of truancy and school suspensions.

TABLE 5-13. Correlates for the A-sch Scale for normative and clinical boys and girls (14-18 years)

Source	Scale or item	Normative sample		Clinical sample	
		Boys	Girls	Boys	Girls
BIO	Number of school problems	.36	.33	.37	.41
BIO	Marks in school	−.37	−.33	−.44	−.44
BIO	Number of school activities	−.19	−.20	−.26	NS
BIO	Course failure in school	NS	−.22	−.29	−.36
BIO	Disciplinary/probation problems in school	NS	.20	−.32	−.28
BIO	Suspension from school	NS	.20	.32	.22
BIO	Repeated grade in school	NS	NS	.24	NS
LE	Suspended from school	.26	.27	.20	.23
LE	Repeated a grade in school	.19	.20	NS	NS
LE	Had an outstanding personal achievement	NS	−.21	NS	NS
LE	Dropped out of school/training program	NS	NS	.19	NS
LE	Increase in disagreements with parent(s)	NS	NS	NS	.28
LE	Caught cheating or lying in school	NS	NS	NS	.18
CBCL	Delinquent	NA	NA	.25	.30
CBCL	Social Competence: School	NA	NA	−.40	−.37
CBCL	Externalizing	NA	NA	NS	.23
RR	Running away	NA	NA	.23	NS
RR	Truancy/School avoidance	NA	NA	.23	.29
RR	Experience with amphetamines	NA	NA	.20	NS
RR	Acting out/Irresponsible behavior	NA	NA	.20	NS
RR	History of being sexually abused	NA	NA	.18	NS
RR	History of learning disabilities	NA	NA	NS	.23
RR	Academic underachievement	NA	NA	NS	.22

Note: BIO refers to Biographical Information Form, LE to Life Events Form, CBCL to Child Behavior Checklist, RR to Record Review. All correlations (r) are Pearson product-moment correlation coefficients with $p \leqslant .0005$ and an absolute magnitude $\geqslant .18$. NS (not significant) indicates the correlate did not reach these significance criteria. NA (not available) indicates that these measures were not collected for the normative subjects.

Among clinical subjects, higher scores also were associated with other acting-out behaviors. Higher-scoring clinical boys were more likely to have had experience with drugs and to have run away from home. Interestingly, higher-scoring clinical boys also were more likely to have histories of having been sexually abused.

In summary, considerable evidence suggests that scores on the A-sch Scale indicate both academic and behavioral problems at school. That the correlates were replicated for boys and girls and for normal

TABLE 5-14. Correlates for the A-trt Scale for normative and clinical boys and girls (14-18 years)

Source	Scale or item	Normative sample		Clinical sample	
		Boys	Girls	Boys	Girls
LE	Gained much weight	NS	.19	NS	.22
LE	Outstanding personal achievement	NS	−.21	NS	NS
LE	Increase in disagreements with parent(s)	NS	NS	NS	.22
RR	Poor social skills	NA	NA	.21	NS

Note: LE refers to Life Events Form, RR to Record Review. All correlations (*r*) are Pearson product-moment correlation coefficients with $p \leq .0005$ and an absolute magnitude $\geq .18$. NS (not significant) indicates the correlate did not reach these significance criteria. NA (not available) indicates that these measures were not collected for the normative subjects.

and clinical subjects increases our confidence in making such inferences about adolescents who score higher on this scale. It also appears that the A-sch Scale assesses general maladjustment. Whether the school problems of higher scorers lead to other symptoms and problem behaviors or vice versa cannot be determined from available data.

Adolescent Negative Treatment Indicators (A-trt)

Our analyses yielded very few significant correlates for the Negative Treatment Indicators (A-trt) Scale for normal or clinical subjects (Table 5-14). There were no significant correlates for normal boys. Normal girls scoring higher on the scale were more likely to report having gained much weight and less likely to report outstanding personal achievements. Records of higher-scoring clinical boys indicated that they were more likely to have poor social skills. Higher-scoring clinical girls were more likely to report having gained much weight and to have experienced increases in disagreements with parents.

The A-trt Scale was meant to assess negative attitudes toward doctors and mental health professionals, feeling unable and/or unwilling to face problems and responsibilities, and feeling uncomfortable talking about problems with others. Unfortunately, data directly relevant to treatment-related attitudes and behaviors were not available for the adolescents that we studied. Therefore, it is not surprising that so few significant correlates were found for the scale. Further research is needed to determine to what extent scores on the scale are related to treatment process and outcome. It is encouraging that in our data scores on the A-trt Scale were not correlated significantly with many problems and symptoms. This suggests that the scale is not simply a measure of general maladjustment.

General Conclusions

Examination of Tables 5-1 through 5-14 reveals several clear trends. For each of the MMPI-A Content Scales, more correlations were significant than would be expected by chance. However, some scales had many more significant correlates than did others. For example, across all the samples, the Cynicism (A-cyn) Scale had no significant correlates, whereas the School Problems (A-sch) Scale had 44 significant correlates (Table 5-13). Although the variation in the number of significant correlates might reflect different degrees of scale validity, it is more likely that it reflects differences in the presence of appropriate criterion measures and in the occurrence of relevant extratest behaviors in the samples studied. For example, many extratest variables and items dealt with school behaviors, but relatively few related to the cynical attitudes assessed by the A-cyn Scale or the treatment-related issues assessed by the Negative Treatment Indicators (A-trt) Scale.

The analyses identified many more significant extratest correlates of the MMPI-A Content Scales for clinical subjects than for normal subjects, largely because fewer extratest measures were available for normal subjects. For normal boys and girls, only the Life Events Form and the Biographical Information Form were available in sufficient numbers to provide adequate power to detect relationships meeting our significance criteria (see Chapter 2). In addition to the life events and biographical forms, teacher, parent, and professional staff ratings and information obtained through record reviews were available for clinical subjects.

The number of significant extratest correlates also could be related to the number of subjects in each sample for whom specific questionnaire and rating scale items were available. For reasons described in Chapter 2, not every subject completed all questionnaire items (or had all items completed by raters). Table 5-15 reports the range of sample sizes utilized in the various analyses conducted to identify extratest correlates. Although these differing sample sizes could have led to minor differences in significance of correlations, it seems unlikely that such differences would affect the overall picture of what a specific MMPI-A Content Scale seems to be assessing.

More significant extratest correlates were identified for girls than for boys in both the normal and clinical samples. This finding is consistent with other research indicating that girls and women typically

TABLE 5-15. Sample sizes used in the validity analyses for normative and clinical boys and girls (14-18 years)

	Normative sample		Clinical sample	
	Boys	Girls	Boys	Girls
Total sample size[a]	805	815	420	293
Interitem variability[b]				
BIO	796-805 (805)	809-815 (815)	312-389 (411)	222-261 (278)
LE	794-804 (805)	802-813 (815)	402-409 (409)	273-277 (277)
CBCL	0	0	214-279 (279)	159-202 (202)
DAB	0	0	313 (313)	221 (221)
RR	0	0	347-412 (412)	262-284 (284)

Note: BIO refers to Biographical Information Form, LE to Life Events Form, CBCL to Child Behavior Checklist, DAB to Devereux Adolescent Behavior Rating Scale, and RR to Record Review.

[a]Total sample size is based on the number of subjects completing an MMPI.

[b]Interitem variability presents the range of subjects who answered individual items on the specified forms. The numbers in parentheses indicate the total subjects who completed the specified forms.

are willing to report more symptoms and psychopathology than are boys and men (in self-reports and in interactions with significant others, such as parents or treatment staff). These greater admissions could lead raters to evaluate girls as having more psychological symptoms than boys. Therefore, the differences in numbers of extratest correlates should not be interpreted as indicating that the content scales have differential validity for boys and girls.

Examination of the data in Tables 5-1 through 5-14 indicates that some of the MMPI-A Content Scales have similar correlates. For example, both the A-con Scale and the A-sch Scale correlated significantly with a variety of problem behaviors in school (e.g., number of school problems, marks in school, disciplinary/probation problems in school, suspension from school). Because these scales have no overlapping items (see Table 3-3), it seems likely that the similarity of correlates is explained by the overlap of the constructs underlying the scales. This interpretation is supported by the relatively high correlations between these scales in the normative samples (i.e., .56 for boys, .58 for girls; see Table 4-7). It is reasonable to expect that adolescents who are acting out will do so in school as well as in other aspects of their lives. However, it is interesting to note that the A-con Scale correlated significantly with several indicators of legal problems (i.e., arrested for stealing, court appearance, court involvement for violent non-status offense) that were not significantly correlated with the A-sch Scale. Thus, an adolescent scoring high on the A-sch Scale but not on the A-con Scale would be likely to act out in the school setting but not necessarily outside of school.

The data discussed in this chapter should be interpreted with some caution. Although the samples were quite large, the extratest information available about subjects was not sufficient to offer a comprehensive test of the validity of all of the content scales. For scales where relevant criterion information was available, the external correlates of the scales were numerous and strong.

Chapter 6

An Interpretive Strategy for the MMPI-A Content Scales

Interpretation of the MMPI-A standard scales relies heavily on inferences about scores that are based on empirical research findings. Because of the empirical manner in which the original MMPI standard scales were constructed, the content of items in these scales is quite heterogeneous. Thus, an individual's elevation on a standard scale might be based on (or explained by) a homogeneous subgroup of the scale's items, and this particular subgroup might be most closely associated with only a portion of the many possible empirically based behavioral correlates for the entire scale. Determining which of the many empirically established correlates apply to any particular individual's scores can be a difficult task for the test interpreter.

For example, according to the MMPI-A manual (Butcher et al., 1992), an elevation on Scale 2 (Depression) is associated with several descriptors in adolescent girls, including depression, social withdrawal, weight gain, having few or no friends, eating problems, low self-esteem, suicidal ideas/gestures, somatic complaints, being unlikely to act out, and being unlikely to be truant or avoid school. Reliance solely on the standard scales does not address which of these descriptors apply to a particular individual.

Harris and Lingoes (1955, 1968) suggest that there are five subgroups of items in Scale 2: subjective depression, psychomotor retardation, physical malfunctioning, mental dullness, and brooding. It seems likely that Scale 2 elevations resulting from endorsement of items in one of these categories could be associated with different behavioral correlates from elevations resulting from endorsement of items in other categories. Harris and Lingoes developed their subscales to be used in this manner. However, the Harris-Lingoes subscales have some notable limitations. Many contain too few items (some as few as six) to serve as reliable psychometric measures of the dimensions being assessed. The Harris-Lingoes subscales provide a limited view of the content dimensions in the MMPI-A because extensive item content was added to the instrument that is not included in the Harris-Lingoes subscales. In addition, Harris and Lingoes developed subscales for only six of the standard scales.

The MMPI-A Content Scales provide a more comprehensive view of the content of an adolescent's test responses in a reliable psychometric format. In the example given above, a clinician could clarify the meaning of a Scale 2 elevation by examining the relevant MMPI-A Content Scale scores (e.g., A-dep, A-lse, A-hea, A-sod, and A-sch). For example, by examining these scores, a clinician could decide how much to emphasize the somatic features or low self-esteem components of Scale 2 elevations.

Although the MMPI-A Content Scales can be used to help clarify the meaning of elevated scores on the standard scales, they can also stand alone as psychometric measures. In Chapter 5 we presented data on the correlates of elevated content scale scores for normal and clinical adolescent subjects. These data can serve as the basis for interpreting elevated content scale scores.

In addition, the MMPI-A Content Scales allow direct communication between the client completing the test and the clinician interpreting it. Assuming that the adolescent responds honestly, scale elevations summarize item content that the individual endorses as personally relevant. The behaviors, problems, and attitudes reflected by elevations on one or more of the 15 MMPI-A Content Scales are those that the adolescent wants to reveal to the examiner. Discussion of test results with adolescents is facilitated if feedback is based on scores on the MMPI-A Content Scales.

An Interpretive Strategy

A comprehensive interpretation of the MMPI-A Content Scales involves the following tasks:

1. Appraise the context in which the testing took place.

2. Assess the test-taking attitudes of the subject.

3. Consider the relative elevations of the content scale scores.

4. Generate inferences about elevated content scale scores.

5. Use the information from the content scales to supplement interpretation of the MMPI-A standard scales.

Butcher and Williams (1992) provide more detailed information about this MMPI-A interpretive strategy.

Appraisal of the Testing Context

The first step in an MMPI-A Content Scale interpretation is to determine the context in which the adolescent completed the instrument and other relevant extratest information. Did the client have an adequate reading level for the test? Was the adolescent sufficiently informed of the reasons for testing? Was the adolescent a willing or an unwilling participant in the testing? Was the adolescent informed of how the results of the testing would be used and with whom they would be shared? Were there reasons for the adolescent to present him- or herself in an overly positive or negative manner? These factors are very important because they can influence the way adolescents respond to the items. As discussed earlier, it is extremely important for an adolescent to be cooperative and honest in responding to the test items if the content scale scores are to reflect important characteristics of the individual accurately.

Assessment of Test-Taking Attitudes

Because the assessment of symptoms and personality characteristics using content-based scales requires optimal cooperation from the test subject, the interpreter must determine whether the MMPI-A test results are valid and if there were any test-taking attitudes that must be considered in interpreting content scale scores. Many adolescents are motivated to acknowledge and describe their problems and behaviors, producing honest and believable self-reports. However, in some clinical applications, adolescents may provide a distorted view of their current adjustment. They may either exaggerate or understate their symptoms and problems. Because content scale scores are vulnerable to response distortion, such attitudes could lead to scores that do not accurately portray the adolescent's behavior and attitudes. The MMPI-A includes several scales that are designed specifically to provide information about the client's test-taking attitudes.

The Cannot Say (?) score is the total number of items left unanswered or answered both true and false by a test subject. It provides an evaluation of the subject's cooperativeness in disclosing personal information. If the adolescent has omitted more than 10 items, cooperation is questionable; if more than 30 items have been omitted, the test results should be considered invalid. The location of omitted responses on the answer sheet is also an important consideration. For example, if they are all in the back of the booklet, after item 350, the standard scales can be scored and interpreted, but the scores on the content scales would likely produce an inaccurate description of the individual. Close supervision of testing is the best way to prevent this response style. The test administrator should encourage subjects to complete any omitted items unless it is determined that poor reading ability is the reason for omissions.

The L and K Scales assess a tendency to claim excessive virtue or to present an overly favorable view of oneself. Such tendencies lead to lower levels of acknowledgment of symptoms and problems and produce generally lower content scale elevations (Lachar & Alexander, 1978). T scores greater than 65 on either the L Scale or the K Scale indicate that the content scales should be interpreted with caution, because their scores may underrepresent the symptoms and problems of test subjects.

The F Scale of the original MMPI was developed to assess random responding resulting from a subject's failure to read the items and respond to their content. Later, it was learned that persons who exaggerated symptoms and problems also produced elevated scores on the F Scale, as did individuals who were accurately reporting severe psychopathology. Problems with the original F Scale with adolescents led to a refinement of this measure in the MMPI-A (Butcher et al., 1992; see also Chapter 1 for a discussion of these changes). The MMPI-A contains three scales to assess the problematic response styles measured by the original F Scale. The F, F1, and F2 Scales of the MMPI-A are all based on the frequency of item endorsements. The F Scale contains 66 items that were endorsed by less than 20% of the adolescent normative sample. F1 and F2 are the first and second halves, respectively, of the F Scale.

In interpreting MMPI-A standard scales, the F1 score is most important, because these scales are scored from responses to items in the first half of the MMPI-A booklet. However, interpretation of the MMPI-A Content Scales requires careful evaluation of both the F1 and F2 scores, since many of the items on the content scales appear toward the end of the test booklet. If an individual produces an elevation on the F1 or F2 Scale greater than a T score of 80, the profile should be examined further to determine its validity. Several possible reasons for infrequent responding need to be considered before the profile is eliminated from interpretive consideration. First, it is possible that the subject has accurately claimed a very broad range of psychological and health symptoms. A second possibility is that the adolescent has simply exaggerated his or her problems in an effort to gain attention. Knowing that either of these motivational conditions exists can aid the clinician in better understanding the adolescent's problem situation. However, another more problematic response set could be operating, the possibility that the individual has randomly or carelessly responded to the items, simply presenting a meaningless pattern of answers.

The random or non-content-oriented response style, which is signaled by elevations on F, F1, and F2, is important to eliminate from consideration, but cannot be excluded on the basis of F elevations alone. The VRIN, or Variable Response Inconsistency Scale, provides another perspective on random responding and helps eliminate this possibility from consideration. VRIN is a response inconsistency scale providing information about whether the individual has responded to the MMPI-A items according to the meaning of the items or simply has endorsed items in a careless or random manner. This scale (and the TRIN Scale, discussed below) was developed by statistically identifying pairs of items that were similar in item content through the use of item intercorrelations. If an individual answers similar items in different (inconsistent) ways, then it is assumed that the subject is not responding carefully to the meaning of the items.

MMPI-A protocols from random responders should not be considered accurate portrayals of their personality characteristics. Thus, if an individual has a large number of VRIN responses (T score greater than 75), it indicates that he or she has responded inconsistently to the items. On the other hand, if an individual who produced a high F, F1, or F2 score responded consistently to the items (i.e., produced a VRIN score within the acceptable range), it would be unlikely that careless or random responding would explain the F elevations.

Also of value in eliminating uninterpretable records from consideration is the TRIN, or True Response Inconsistency Scale. This scale measures whether an individual has responded consistently to similar items that are keyed in the same direction (i.e., either both true or both false). If the individual answers a large number of TRIN items in the false direction (i.e., T score ≥75), a "nay-saying" response set is suggested. If a large number of items are endorsed in the true direction, a "yea-saying" response set is suggested. Before the MMPI-A Content Scales are considered interpretable, the subject's response approach should be determined to be internally consistent—that is, to have TRIN and VRIN scores in the acceptable range.

Careful evaluation of the above validity scales will provide important information about the credibility of the test subject's self-disclosure, enabling a clinician to determine how much confidence to place in the interpretation of the MMPI-A Content Scales. Obviously, if the subject has responded to the items in a clearly invalid manner, the content scales, as well as any other MMPI-A scale, should not be interpreted. If the subject has exaggerated or minimized symptoms and problems to some extent, the content scale scores will be artificially high or low. Most confidence should be placed on content scores in a test protocol where the subject has responded validly and has not exaggerated or minimized problems. Butcher and Williams (1992) detail these interpretive guidelines.

Generation of Inferences from Content Scales

Inferences can be generated about a test subject based on scores on the 15 MMPI-A Content Scales. Uniform T scores should be used for this purpose. Uniform T scores assure that a given T score has the same percentile equivalent for each content scale. For example, a uniform T score of 65 falls at a percentile rank of 92 for all scales. The Adolescent MMPI Project Committee recommended that uniform T scores of 65 or higher on the clinical scales of MMPI-A be considered clinically significant. However, that committee also recommended that uniform T scores between 60 and 64 be considered as suggestive of clinical or personality problems that need further assessment (Butcher et al., 1992). We recommend these same T-score cutoffs for the MMPI-A Content Scales.

The narrative descriptions that follow for the various content scales can be used as sources of inferences about test subjects. Any uniform T score of 60 or greater should lead to inferences. However, greater emphasis should be placed on inferences based on more elevated scores. Whereas a T score between 60 and 64 may suggest that a test subject might have certain problems or characteristics, we would have more confidence in their existence if the T score were considerably more elevated (e.g., 80 or higher). At present, very little is known about the meaning of low scores on the content scales. Low scores indicate that the individual has not acknowledged having problems in that particular content domain.

The descriptions of individuals with high scores on the MMPI-A Content Scales are based on several sources of data, including both item meanings and scale correlates. Because the content scales are much more homogeneous than the clinical scales, examination of their item content can provide important information about test subjects. However, it should be understood that not all high scorers will have endorsed all items in a scale in the scored direction. Correlations between content scales and the more established validity and clinical scales of MMPI-A provide additional information about the meaning of scores on the content scales (see Chapter 4). Finally, the correlate data presented in Chapter 5 provide a rich source of information about the meaning of higher scores on the various content scales. It should be recognized that not every significant correlate for a scale will apply to every person who obtains a high score on the scale. Taken together, these various data sources permit us to generate some preliminary descriptions of high scorers. These descriptions will be expanded, and in some cases amended, as additional data become available.

Adolescent Anxiety (A-anx). Adolescents who obtain high scores on the A-anx Scale are reporting many symptoms of anxiety. These symptoms may include tension, excessive worry, or sleep disturbance. High scorers also may be reporting problems in concentrating and attending, and at times they may be confused. Girls scoring high on this scale tend to have somatic symptoms and feel depressed. High scorers on this scale often report increased disagreements with their parents. High scorers are likely to be aware of their difficulties, may feel that life is a strain much of the time, and may believe that their difficulties are so great that they will not be able to overcome them.

Adolescent Obsessiveness (A-obs). High scorers on the A-obs Scale are reporting that they worry a great deal, often about very trivial matters. They may be reporting that "bad words" come into their minds, that they count unimportant items, or that they have difficulty sleeping because of worries. Also, high scorers may be reporting difficulty making decisions or dread making changes in their lives. They may be reporting that others sometimes lose patience with them. Boys who score high on the scale are overly passive and dependent in relationships with adults and tend to blame themselves for perceived bad behavior. Girls who score high on the scale may have histories of suicidal ideas and/or gestures.

Adolescent Depression (A-dep). High scorers on the A-dep Scale are reporting symptoms of depression. They may be reporting sadness, fatigue, crying spells, and self-deprecatory thoughts. They may describe life as uninteresting and not worthwhile and report feelings of loneliness, pessimism, and uselessness. High scorers tend to have histories of suicidal ideas and/or gestures. They tend not to be very active, and they are likely to be socially introverted. Boys who score high on the scale may have histories of having been sexually abused. Girls who score high on the scale tend to have passive and dependent relationships with adults and typically do poorly in school.

Adolescent Health Concerns (A-hea). Adolescents who score high on the A-hea Scale are reporting somatic symptoms and concerns about health. Complaints may include gastrointestinal difficulties (e.g., nausea, vomiting, constipation), neurological difficulties (e.g., numbness, dizziness, fainting or dizzy spells, paralysis), sensory problems (e.g., poor eyesight, hearing impairment), cardiovascular symptoms (e.g., heart or chest pain), pain (headaches, neck pain), or respiratory problems. High scorers tend to be internalizers. Academic and behavioral problems in school are common among them. High-scoring boys are described as guilty, fearful, clinging, worrying, and hearing things. High-scoring girls report increased disagreements with parents.

Adolescent Bizarre Mentation (A-biz). High scorers on the A-biz Scale are reporting strange thoughts and experiences, which may include hallucinations, persecutory ideas, or feelings of being controlled by others. High scorers in clinical settings are likely to be described by others as displaying psychotic behaviors such as bizarre sensory experiences, disturbed speech, mannerisms, or strange and grandiose ideas about themselves. High scorers often seem to believe that there is something wrong with their minds. They often are from families in which arguments, arrests, and perhaps even child abuse occur. Among normal adolescents, higher scorers typically perform poorly in school and are involved in various kinds of misbehavior.

Adolescent Anger (A-ang). Adolescents with high scores on the A-ang Scale typically are reporting anger control problems. They tend to report swearing, smashing things, or starting fights. They may indicate that they are irritable and impatient with others and may throw temper tantrums to get their own way. High-scoring boys tend to be passive, dependent, and clinging in relationships with adults, and their histories may include indications of sexual abuse. High scorers tend to be involved in acting-out behavior, including aggressive or assaultive acts, and may have been in trouble at school and with the law. High-scoring girls report strong heterosexual interests.

Adolescent Cynicism (A-cyn). High scorers on the A-cyn Scale have endorsed items indicating misanthropic attitudes. They seem to be questioning the motives of other people. They are indicating that it is better to trust nobody. They are feeling misunderstood and mistreated. Preliminary data have not yielded significant extratest correlates for this scale, but this may be because appropriate descriptors were not included in the instruments used in the research.

Adolescent Alienation (A-aln). High scorers on the A-aln Scale are reporting emotional distance from other people. They may be indicating that other people do not like, understand, or care about them. They may be reporting difficulty in talking to other people, especially about themselves. They may be indicating that they do not have as much fun as other adolescents seem to have. High scorers tend to have poor academic performance. Boys who score high on the scale have histories of low self-esteem and poor social skills, and they deny having used alcohol or other drugs. Girls who score high on the scale tend to have concerns about weight gain and disagreements with parents. High-scoring girls are likely to have histories of few or no friends.

Adolescent Conduct Problems (A-con). High scorers on the A-con Scale are likely to be reporting behavioral problems including stealing, shoplifting, lying, breaking or destroying things, being disrespectful, swearing, or being oppositional. They may be indicating that their peer groups often are in trouble and that their friends often talk them into doing things they know they should not do. High scorers have histories of poor academic performance and behavioral problems in school that have led to disciplinary actions and/or suspension from school. They tend to have problems with alcohol or other drugs. High-scoring boys may have histories of running away from home, and high-scoring girls may have histories of having been sexually active.

Adolescent Low Self-Esteem (A-lse). Adolescents with high scores on the A-lse Scale are expressing very negative opinions of themselves. They may be describing themselves as unattractive, lacking in self-confidence, feeling useless, having little ability, or not being able to do anything very well. They may be indicating that they are easily influenced by others and they do not feel capable of solving their own problems or planning their own futures. High scorers have histories of low self-esteem. Boys who score high on this scale have poor social skills and may have histories of having been sexually abused. Girls who score high on this scale may have histories of poor school performance, depression, and suicidal ideas and/or gestures.

Adolescent Low Aspirations (A-las). High scorers on the A-las Scale are indicating little interest in being successful and do not expect to be successful. They may be reporting that they do not like to read and study about things, prefer work that allows them to be careless, and are seen as lazy by others. They may be reporting that they have difficulty starting things, give up quickly when things go wrong, and let other people solve problems for them. High scorers typically have poor academic performance, participate in few school activities, and have multiple school problems.

Adolescent Social Discomfort (A-sod). Adolescents who score high on the A-sod Scale are reporting discomfort in social situations. They are indicating that they have difficulty making friends and initiating conversation with other people and that they tend to avoid parties, dances, and other social gatherings. High scorers on the scale tend to be socially withdrawn and to have few or no friends. Girls who score high on the scale may indicate that they are depressed and have eating problems, are not very interested in boys, do not use alcohol or drugs, and do not engage in irresponsible behavior.

Adolescent Family Problems (A-fam). High scorers on the A-fam Scale are reporting numerous problems with parents and other family members. They may be characterizing their families as angry, jealous, faultfinding, physically abusive, lacking in love and understanding, or unable to communicate effectively. They may be indicating that they cannot count on their families in times of trouble and are looking forward to the day when they are able to leave home. High scorers report increasing disagreements with their parents and worsening arguments between their parents. They tend to have poor academic performance and school problems of various kinds. In clinical settings, high scorers tend to have histories of delinquent, hostile, and aggressive behavior. Interestingly, they also tend to display neurotic behaviors such as internalizing, dependency, and withdrawal. Boys scoring high on the scale may have histories of being physically abused, and girls scoring high on the scale may have histories of being sexually abused.

Adolescent School Problems (A-sch). High scorers on the A-sch Scale are reporting various kinds of difficulties in school. They may be indicating that the only positive aspect of school is interacting with friends and that school is a waste of time. Some high scorers may be reporting that they are afraid to go to school. High scorers on the scale have poor academic performance, tend not to participate in school activities, and may have histories of truancy and suspension from school. High-scoring boys also tend to be involved in acting-out behaviors outside of school. They may have histories of alcohol and drug involvement and of running away from home. Interestingly, high-scoring boys also may have histories of having been sexually abused.

Adolescent Negative Treatment Indicators (A-trt). The A-trt Scale was developed to assess attitudes toward mental health problems and professionals that would interfere with psychological interventions. High scorers on the scale seem to be indicating that others cannot understand their problems and really do not care what happens to them. They may be saying that they feel uncomfortable sharing personal things with others. They may be indicating an unwillingness to accept responsibility for the negative things in their lives or to take charge and face their problems and difficulties. Preliminary research has not revealed many external correlates for the A-trt Scale. This may reflect the absence of appropriate items in the research instruments. Additional research is needed to determine the extent to which this scale fulfills its intended purpose.

Sometimes the inferences made from the individual MMPI-A Content Scales are not internally consistent. For example, a test subject might have elevated scores on both the A-con Scale, suggesting substance abuse, and on A-sod, suggesting a more introverted and socially isolated person with a lesser likelihood of substance abuse. Some attempt must be made to decide which of the inconsistent inferences is more likely to be accurate for this test subject. In general, early research with the MMPI suggests that descriptors of externalizing or acting-out behaviors may be more salient than the internalizing symptoms, and thus should be given more emphasis. Although often the scores on the two scales leading to the inconsistent inferences will be elevated significantly (i.e., above 65), one scale may be much more elevated than the other. More confidence should be placed in the inferences derived from more elevated scales. Also, some inferences about elevated scores are based on the item content of scales, whereas other inferences are based on external validity studies.

Supplementing Interpretation of Standard Scales

As stated earlier in this chapter, the MMPI-A Content Scales can be used in two major ways. They can provide information concerning which of the many correlates suggested for a standard scale should be emphasized for a particular individual. They also can be used to generate inferences about individuals in areas that are not addressed adequately by the standard scales.

When a score is elevated on a standard scale of MMPI-A, the various descriptors suggested for that scale in the MMPI-A manual should be considered. Often a rather wide variety of symptoms and other behaviors will be suggested. By noting which content scales also are elevated, a clinician can determine which symptoms should be emphasized for a particular case. For example, an elevated Scale 4 score for an adolescent boy would be suggestive of many correlates, including some having to do with delinquent and acting-out behaviors, but also some having to do with dependent behaviors and poor social competence. If the boy had an elevated score on the Adolescent Conduct Disorders (A-con) Scale but not on Adolescent Low Self-Esteem (A-lse) or Adolescent Social Discomfort (A-sod), one would emphasize the acting-out correlates and not those having to do with dependence and social discomfort. Conversely, if the boy did not have an elevated score on A-con but had elevated scores on A-lse and/or A-sod, the correlates having to do with dependence and social discomfort should be emphasized.

Information from the content scales can also be used to address more directly issues and behaviors not directly assessed by the standard scales. For example, the standard scales do not address directly family problems, low aspirations, low self-esteem, anger, or treatment potential. The inferences based on the content scales having to do with these areas of functioning could add significantly to those based on the standard scales.

Case Illustrations

The three cases selected to illustrate the interpretation of the MMPI-A Content Scales were obtained from samples collected in the adolescent treatment settings described in Chapter 2. Research files on each adolescent included a great deal of information, such as record reviews, the Child Behavior Checklist, Devereux Adolescent Behavior Rating Scale, Youth Self-Report, Teacher Report Form, and Diagnostic Interview for Children and Adolescents. Some files also included notes giving research assistants' impressions of the adolescents based on their interactions. Those who generated the information in the research files did not know the subject's MMPI-A results. These cases are presented primarily to illustrate how the MMPI-A Content Scales can be used in conjunction with the validity and standard scales.

CASE 1: TRACY

Background

Age: 16

Grade: 11

Gender: girl

Ethnicity: white

Setting: inpatient psychiatric unit

Referral Concerns. Tracy was admitted to an inpatient psychiatric unit after a suicide attempt (her first). At admission she was seen as depressed and having low-self esteem related to a number of recent stressors. She had been sexually assaulted, beaten up, and in an accident that left scars. She reported that her father had physically abused her since mid-adolescence. Tracy had a child born out of wedlock who lived with her parents. She expressed fear that her father would harm the child. Tracy reported the arrest of a parent and a sibling within the last six months and indicated that family discord was worsening. Family problems were prominent, and she was somewhat oppositional and impulsive.

Diagnostic Impressions. The admitting clinician suggested that Tracy was experiencing an adjustment reaction (to the sexual assault) with depressed mood. Her discharge diagnosis was also adjustment disturbance with depressed mood.

Symptoms and Behavior in the Hospital. The treatment staff described Tracy as difficult to get to know and distant from both staff and peers on her unit. During a computer-administered interview, Tracy admitted to psychotic behaviors, including hallucinations, strange body sensations, and delusional thinking. However, hospital records did not indicate such psychotic behaviors during hospitalization. During the interview Tracy also admitted to current suicidal ideas and alcohol and marijuana use. She said that she was fearful of her father. Tracy was discharged from the hospital after three days to the custody of an older sibling. Records did not indicate the reasons for such a brief hospital stay.

Interpretation of Validity and Standard MMPI-A Scales. Tracy approached the MMPI-A in a frank and open manner, as reflected in her low L and K Scale scores and her slightly elevated F Scale scores. Although she admitted to a significant number of symptoms and problems, such admission was consistent with her inpatient status. VRIN and TRIN average scores indicate no problems with inconsistent responding. Her cooperative approach resulted in a clearly valid and interpretable set of scores and was maintained throughout the test, as indicated by the similar level of scores for both the F1 and F2 Scales. Thus, both the standard scales and content scales are likely to be valid estimates of current psychological functioning.

The elevations on several standard scales (Scales 4, 6, 7, 8, 9, 0) suggest that Tracy is experiencing significant psychological problems. Considerable emotional turmoil, including anxiety and depression, is suggested by elevations on Scales 7 and 0. Tracy is also likely to be shy, introverted, and withdrawn, given these elevations. She may be rather rigid, perfectionistic, and self-critical. Her Scale 0 elevation further suggests the possibility of suicidal ideas and perhaps attempts. Significant elevations on Scales 6 and 8 raise the possibility of a thought disorder. Confused and disorganized thinking, delusions, and halluci-

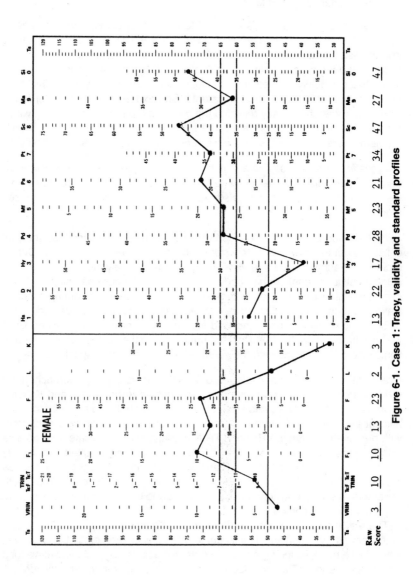

Figure 6-1. Case 1: Tracy, validity and standard profiles

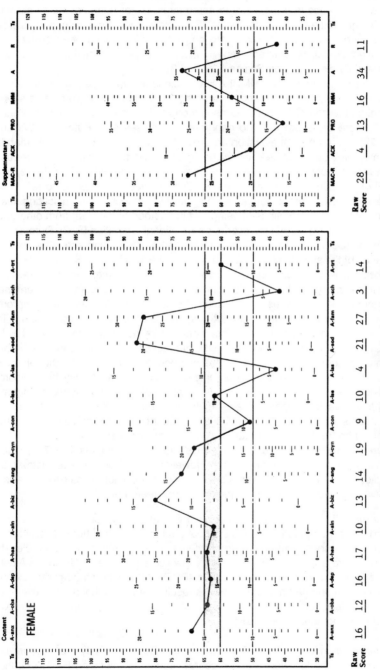

Figure 6-2. Case 1: Tracy, content and supplementary profiles

nations may be present. It is not possible from available data to know whether this disturbance is a response to acute stressors or a long-standing problem, although studies with the original MMPI would support the latter hypothesis. Her elevations on Scales 4 and 8 are consistent with having been sexually assaulted. Anger, resentment, rebellion, and acting-out behavior are also suggested by elevations on Scales 4, 6, and 8.

An examination of her MMPI-A Harris-Lingoes and Scale 0 subscale scores for her most prominent standard scales (i.e., Scales 4, 6, 8, 0) reveals several content themes. Only those Harris-Lingoes subscale elevations that are above a T score of 65 are used to generate hypotheses (see Butcher & Williams, 1992). Her prominent elevation on Scale 4 appears to result from considerable family problems and feelings of being alienated from others; she produced prominent subscale elevations on Family Problems (Pd1), Social Alienation (Pd4), and Self-Alienation (Pd5). Her Scale 6 elevation appears to reflect two content areas, Persecutory Ideas (Pa1) and Poignancy (Pa2), indicating suspicion, distrust, and feelings of being misunderstood and distant from others. On Scale 8 she produced high scores on Emotional Alienation (Sc2), Defective Inhibition (Sc5), and Bizarre Sensory Experiences (Sc6), supporting the extreme nature of the symptoms. Finally, on Scale 0 she was high on Shyness (Si1) and Social Avoidance (Si2), indicating discomfort around others and withdrawal.

In summary, her MMPI-A standard scale elevations appear to be determined, in large part, by themes such as loss of emotional control, unusual symptoms, family problems, alienation from others, and self-alienation. Diagnostically, Tracy's symptoms and problems seem more severe than would be indicated by her diagnosis of adjustment disorder with depressed mood. Her pattern of scores on the standard scales raises concerns about the presence of a thought disorder. The possibility of a schizophrenic disorder or an acute psychotic disorder should be explored carefully. The high degree of emotional distress suggested by the elevations on the F Scale and some of the standard scales, coupled with concerns about suicide potential and thought disorder, suggests that Tracy should be treated in a structured environment where she will feel safe and secure. Her willingness to express distress and other symptoms (F, 6, 7, 8) is seen as a positive indicator for treatment. However, her suspiciousness, distrust, and difficulty in forming meaningful relationships with others (Scales 6, 8, and 0) have negative implications for psychological treatment.

Interpretation of Alcohol/Drug Problem Scales. Tracy's scores on the alcohol and other drug problem scales suggest a mixed picture of her potential for developing serious alcohol or drug problems. Although she obtained an elevated MAC score at 70, she obtained a very low score (T score of 41) on the Alcohol and Drug Problem Proneness Scale (PRO). Moreover, she clearly acknowledged that she had not had problems resulting from alcohol or drug use in the item content, reflected by her T score of 51 on the Alcohol and Drug Problem Acknowledgment Scale (ACK).

Interpretation of MMPI-A Content Scales. Because Tracy was cooperative throughout the test (low L and K scores; some elevations on F, F1, F2), interpretation of the content scales is appropriate. Elevations on several of the content scales reinforce impressions formed from the clinical scales. The very high A-biz score is an additional reason to be concerned about a thought disorder. A-biz elevations tend to be associated with delusions, hallucinations, and bizarre sensory experiences. Elevations on A-anx and A-sod are indicative of anxiety, depression, and other emotional turmoil. The very high A-sod score supports inferences that Tracy is shy, timid, and socially uncomfortable. A significantly elevated A-cyn score reinforces the impression that Tracy questions the motives of others and finds it difficult to trust others.

The scores on the content scales also help to resolve some inconsistencies in inferences based on the clinical scales. The average scores on A-con and A-sch indicate that Tracy is not likely to be acting out in ways that get her into trouble at school or with the law. The very high A-fam score suggests that Tracy is experiencing very serious family problems and may act out to some extent in the home environment.

The content scale scores also add important information about Tracy. Her very elevated A-fam score gives a much clearer picture of her negative family environment. She is likely to feel that she cannot count on her family in times of great need. The A-fam elevation also is consistent with other available information suggesting that the home environment is in considerable turmoil. Girls who score high on A-fam sometimes report having been sexually abused.

The elevation on the A-ang Scale leads to inferences of problems with anger control and, coupled with the elevated A-fam score, suggests that the primary problems with anger are related to family interactions. Because the A-trt Scale is moderately elevated, one can infer that Tracy may not be receptive to the idea of psychological therapy. Her relatively high A-cyn score indicates that she does not see others as being understanding and helpful, and thus may have difficulty developing a trusting relationship with a therapist.

Comments. The MMPI-A Content Scales supplement the interpretation of the validity and standard scales. In many ways, the content scale scores reinforce impressions based on the standard scales (e.g., depression, suicide, thought disorder). The content scale scores also help to resolve some inconsistencies in inferences based on the standard scales (e.g., whether or not Tracy is likely to act out). Finally, the content scales offer important additional information about Tracy (e.g., the severe family problems).

CASE 2: JASON

Background

Age: 14

Grade: 8

Gender: boy

Ethnicity: American Indian

Setting: special school for students with emotional and behavioral problems

Referral Concerns. Although very bright and far above grade level in math and science, Jason had a number of behavior problems that prevented his being educated in a regular classroom or even in a special education classroom within a regular school. During the previous six months he had been caught lying and stealing and had been suspended from school. Jason was the oldest child in his family. He reported that his mother, who recently had been arrested, had beaten him when he was much younger. At the time of the evaluation he was living with an aunt and uncle and reported no problems in their home.

Diagnostic Impressions. Diagnoses were not routinely assigned in Jason's school, so there was no indication of a current diagnosis in his school records. However, his responses to the computer-administered diagnostic interview that was part of our research project strongly suggested a conduct disorder. He met criteria for both oppositional disorder and conduct disorder, undersocialized, aggressive type. During the computer-administered interview Jason admitted that he started drinking alcohol at age 10 and currently used marijuana.

Behavior in School. Jason's teacher, who felt she knew him very well after having had him in class more than five hours a day for seven months, described him as very bright, sensitive, and softhearted. He was physically active, often needing to run outside. He usually excelled at school subjects when he applied himself. He expressed a desire to attend a four-year college. Although he was a perfectionist at times, he hated to correct his school work. His teacher reported that he often stood so close to her that it made her feel uncomfortable. In addition to her positive comments, his teacher also described him as immature, argumentative, defiant, cruel, demanding, disobedient, disruptive, impulsive, explosive, irresponsible, stubborn, moody, and loud. School records indicated that he was involved in fights and often acted out in angry, impulsive ways. He was disliked by many other students and was frequently teased by them. He often seemed to be daydreaming and occasionally expressed feelings of inferiority.

Interpretation of Validity and Standard MMPI-A Scales. The MMPI-A validity scales were within the normal range, suggesting that Jason approached the test in a valid manner. However, his L Scale T score of 63 indicated that he may have tried to present an overly favorable image of himself. He claimed more positive qualities than most adolescents. In spite of this tendency, he admitted to some problems and symptoms as reflected in his score on the F1 Scale. However, both VRIN and TRIN revealed no tendencies toward inconsistent responding.

Jason's scores on the MMPI-A standard scales were well within normal limits. The quite low scores on some of the standard scales could have been a product of his desire to project a positive image. Scores on the standard scales were not suggestive of anxiety, depression, or other emotional turmoil. Likewise, the standard scales did not offer evidence of antisocial or acting-out behavior. The absence of elevations on Scales 6 and 8 suggested that psychotic symptoms and characteristics were not present. The average score on Scale 0 could be interpreted as indicating that Jason was not particularly shy or socially with-

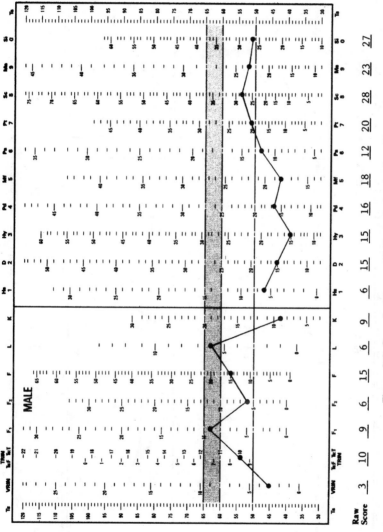

Figure 6-3. Case 2: Jason, validity and standard profiles

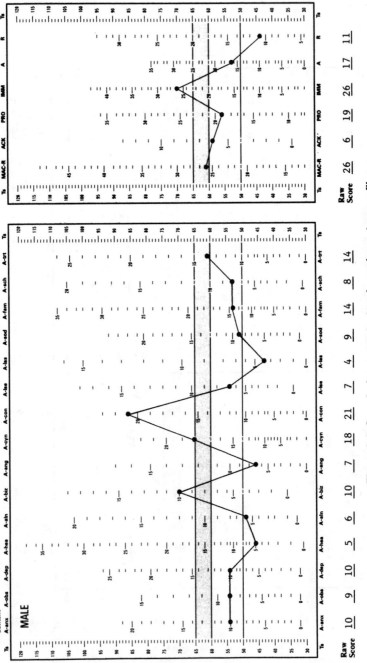

Figure 6-4. Case 2: Jason, content and supplementary profiles

drawn. Since his MMPI-A standard scales were in the normal range, interpretation of the Harris-Lingoes and Si subscales is not recommended.

Based on the validity and standard scale scores alone, it would not be appropriate to assign a psychiatric diagnosis. Knowing that Jason has had numerous behavioral and conduct problems, we would infer from the clinical scales that these problems were not the product of emotional or psychological problems. The absence of elevations on the standard scales that would indicate emotional turmoil (especially Scales 2 and 7) suggests that Jason would not be particularly motivated for psychological treatment.

Interpretation of Alcohol/Drug Problem Scales. His scores on the MAC (moderate elevation of 61) and PRO (T = 56) suggest a slight risk for developing substance abuse problems. His score on ACK (T = 59) suggests less alcohol and other drug problem acknowledgment than many boys in substance abuse treatment programs.

Interpretation of MMPI-A Content Scales. Jason approached the test in a valid manner, so his content scales are interpretable. That both F1 and F2 scores were within normal limits suggests that he was cooperative throughout the test. As noted earlier, his L Scale score was relatively high, suggesting that he tended to present himself in an unrealistically favorable way. This tendency could lead to attenuation of some or all of the content scale scores.

Whereas Jason's standard scale scores were all within normal limits, he had significant elevations on three of the content scales. These elevations permit inferences about Jason that were not possible from the standard scales. The extremely high T score on the A-con Scale suggests serious conduct problems. Adolescent boys who score high on this scale tend to have histories of difficulties at school and with the law. They often have been suspended from school and have been involved with the courts because of violent behavior. They typically report having used alcohol and other substances. High scorers on the A-con Scale typically come from very unstable families, and our research has indicated that child protection workers may have been assigned to their families.

The relatively high score (T = 65) on the A-cyn Scale indicates that Jason seemed to be questioning the motives of others. He may have felt misunderstood and mistreated, and he may have decided that it is better to trust nobody.

The elevated score (T = 70) on the A-biz Scale is difficult to interpret. On the surface it would suggest that Jason may have been experiencing symptoms of a thought disorder such as hallucinations, delusions, or bizarre sensory experiences. Since there were no indicators of such behavior in the standard scales and other information about Jason did not suggest psychotic symptoms, we would be reluctant to infer such symptoms with much confidence. However, the elevated A-biz score should be seen as an indicator that more information about the possibility of a thought disorder should be obtained. Another possibility is that the elevated A-biz score could be associated with drug use.

The content scales suggest that a conduct disorder diagnosis should be considered. Such a diagnosis seems to be in keeping with what we found out about Jason from his teacher and school records and from him in the diagnostic interview. A thought disorder should be ruled out. The content scales do not add much to the clinical scales in terms of implications for treatment. The content scales that would indicate emotional turmoil were not elevated. Elevations on the A-con and A-cyn Scales suggest that Jason would have considerable difficulty trusting others enough to confide in them, and that he would be likely to blame others for his problems.

Comments. This case is a good illustration of a situation in which the content scales permit inferences about an adolescent when the standard scales are all within normal limits. From Jason's standard scale scores we would not have found support in the MMPI-A for conceptualizing Jason's problems primarily as products of a conduct disorder. By contrast, his content scale scores strongly support such a conceptualization. In addition, the elevation on the A-biz Scale alerted us that more information should be obtained concerning the possibility of a thought disorder.

CASE 3: MARK

Background

Age: 17

Grade: 10 (currently not in school)

Gender: boy

Ethnicity: white

Setting: inpatient drug and alcohol unit

Referral Concerns. Mark's use of alcohol and marijuana led to his referral for an inpatient evaluation. Mark had two prior hospitalizations for treatment of substance abuse. He recently was arrested for DWI following an accident. Mark had several incarcerations in juvenile detention facilities and had been in court because of probation violations. Mark's mother died when he was 8 years old. His father remarried, and at the time of his hospitalization he lived with his father, stepmother, and one of his siblings. He reported much quarreling among family members, and he stated concerns that he might hurt his father. Mark dropped out of school after having been expelled or suspended. In school he had earned average grades, and he stated an intention of finishing school and attending a two-year college.

Diagnostic Impressions. At both hospital admission and discharge, Mark's diagnoses involved abuse of alcohol and marijuana. The same diagnoses were suggested by the computerized diagnostic interview, and in that interview Mark also admitted using inhalants, cocaine, hallucinogens, and opiates. During the computerized interview Mark also admitted to a variety of fears, such as being in high places, speaking in front of many people, and his parents being hurt or dying. He also indicated that he felt that he had to touch things repeatedly and that he was troubled by unpleasant thoughts.

Behavior in the Hospital. The treatment staff described Mark as resistant to their requests and persistent when told not to do something. He became easily angered and had considerable difficulty controlling his anger. Although he was dominated by his peers on the unit, he stayed on the fringe of their activities. On the other hand, he sought out the staff for approval and praise. The staff felt that Mark did not understand how he related to them. Mark completed the treatment program in five weeks and was discharged to his parents' home with a referral for aftercare.

Interpretation of Validity and Standard MMPI-A Scales. Mark approached the MMPI-A in a cooperative and open manner. Although he admitted to a large number of symptoms and problems, the scores on the validity scales, including the inconsistency scales VRIN and TRIN, indicated that the other scores were interpretable. Because both the F1 and F2 Scale scores were within acceptable limits, both the standard clinical scales and the content scales could be interpreted.

Mark's only significantly elevated score on the clinical scales was for Scale 4 (T = 72). This elevation suggested that Mark is likely to be involved in a variety of delinquent and acting-out behaviors. Adolescents who score high on this scale tend to have behavior and academic problems at school, sometimes having been suspended from school. They also are likely to be in conflict with their families. They feel rebellious toward parents, tend to argue with parents, and may run away from home. High scorers on Scale 4 sometimes report having been sexually abused.

The elevation on Scale 4 indicated that Mark tends to externalize blame for problems and difficulties, accepting little responsibility for his own behavior. Mark is likely to be socially extroverted and comfortable interacting with others. Adolescents who score high on Scale 4 often receive conduct disorder diagnoses. The only Scale 4 Harris-Lingoes subscale that is in the interpretable range is Authority Problems (Pd2), at a T score of 67. This suggests that Mark endorses considerable resentment toward society, has had several legal problems, and has not fully accepted the standards of society.

Interpretation of Alcohol/Drug Problem Scales. The relatively high scores on the three alcohol problem scales (MAC elevation of 70, ACK T score = 67, and PRO T score = 71) were consistent with a history of substance abuse problems. Because Mark does not accept responsibility for his problems, he may not be motivated to involve himself in a treatment program in order to change. However, substance abuse treatment, perhaps focusing on behavioral control, is necessary given the serious nature of his problems.

Interpretation of MMPI-A Content Scales. Mark's scores on the content scales reinforce some of the inferences made from the clinical scales and also add new insights into his problems. The moderately elevated score (T = 62) on the A-fam Scale reinforces the impression that Mark is likely to be in conflict with his family. It suggests that he sees his family as not very understanding or supportive and that there are likely to be arguments among family members, including Mark. Concern about possible sexual and/or physical abuse, which was inferred from the Scale 4 elevation, is also suggested by the A-fam and A-dep scores.

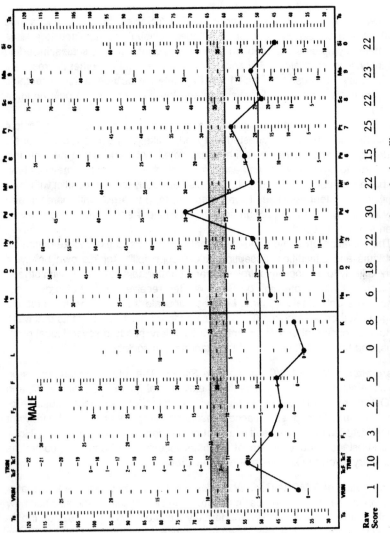

Figure 6-5. Case 3: Mark, validity and standard profiles

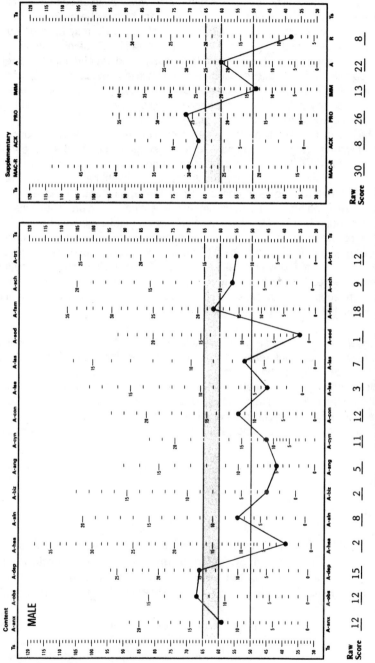

Figure 6-6. Case 3: Mark, content and supplementary profiles

Elevated scores on A-obs (T = 67) and A-dep (T = 62) suggest that Mark is experiencing more distress and discomfort than would be inferred from his clinical scale scores. The A-obs score indicates that he may be worrying excessively and having difficulty sleeping because of worry. He may have difficulty making decisions and may keep at things until others lose patience with him. In relationships with adults he may be rather passive and dependent, often seeking approval and assurances that he is a worthwhile person. The A-dep score indicates that Mark may at times feel sad or unhappy, and may think about suicide. He is likely to feel lonely, pessimistic, and useless. Life does not seem interesting or worthwhile much of the time.

The absence of significantly elevated scores on A-con and A-sch is not consistent with the diagnosis of conduct disorder suggested by Mark's Scale 4 elevations. Based on the content scale scores, one could hypothesize that Mark's acting-out behavior, including his substance abuse, might be motivated by factors other than rebellion and nonconformity. Perhaps he acts out as a way of gaining attention from adults in his life and uses alcohol and drugs as a way of trying to reduce some of the psychological turmoil that he experiences.

The content scale scores also lead to somewhat more optimistic inferences about treatment. To the extent that Mark feels worried and depressed, he will be more motivated to involve himself in a treatment program in order to feel better. If some intervention with his family could lead to reduced disruption in the home and more supportive responses to positive behaviors, some of his distress and acting-out behaviors might change.

Comments. This case is a good example of how the MMPI-A Content Scales can reinforce some inferences that were made from the standard scales and lead to new insights about a person's problems and behaviors. The content scales scores suggested that Mark was experiencing more discomfort and turmoil than the standard scales indicated. In addition, the absence of elevations on A-con and A-sch suggested that Mark's behavior may be motivated by factors other than rebellion and failure to incorporate societal standards and values.

Summary

The goals of this chapter have been to provide an interpretive strategy for the MMPI-A Content Scales, to summarize information relevant to interpretation of the content scales, and to illustrate how to interpret the content scales, along with other MMPI-A based measures, with case examples.

The interpretive strategy recommended here begins with the need to ensure the validity of the protocol before interpretation proceeds. Use of several MMPI-A validity measures was highlighted. We showed two uses of content scale inferences. The first indicated how the interpretation of the empirically derived clinical scales could be refined by examining the content scales. The MMPI-A Content Scales also provided unique information sometimes not available from the standard scales.

The meanings of the MMPI-A Content Scales were summarized, bringing in information both from item content and from the empirical correlates for the scales presented in greater detail in Chapter 5. Interpretation of the different sources of information contained in the MMPI-A (standard scales, supplementary scales such as MAC, ACK, and PRO, and MMPI-A Content Scales) was illustrated with three cases from adolescent treatment settings.

Closing Comments

We undertook the development of content-based scales for the MMPI-A because content interpretation in personality assessment has demonstrated both relevance and effectiveness in addressing important clinical problems in adults. Over the last 20 years the content approach has gained in both popularity and respect. The development of the MMPI-2 Content Scales provided a reliable and valid means of summarizing and understanding what adults tell us about their problems as they respond to the test items. Content scales, in effect, provide a means of psychometrically appraising direct communications between patient and clinician.

Little research has been conducted on the use of content-based measures with adolescents. However, there are no reasons to believe that this approach will not work as well with adolescents as with adults. In fact, the openness with which many adolescents approach personality testing suggests that content-based scales might be particularly useful in understanding their problems. Test defensiveness, which is very much a part of many adult evaluations (e.g., child custody, personnel screening), is not very prominent in most adolescent assessment situations. Rather, when test-taking attitude is of concern, it usually involves symptom and problem exaggeration. However, the MMPI-A has several validity measures designed to help assess this response tendency.

In this book we have explored the content interpretation approach to the clinical assessment of adolescents with the MMPI-A. We are very encouraged that the MMPI-A Content Scales can provide valuable information about adolescents. We found that some of the content dimensions identified in the MMPI-2 replicated well with adolescent samples. These dimensions, such as anxiety, depression, and anger, appear to operate very much as they do with adult samples. Moreover, scales based on these dimensions have similar correlates for adolescents and adults.

In addition to the common content dimensions that the MMPI-A shares with the MMPI-2, some problem areas are unique to adolescents. These content dimensions, such as conduct problems, school problems, low aspirations, and alienation, to a large extent reflect the content domains that were added to the MMPI-A item pool. Scales based on these newer dimensions were shown to have clear and meaningful external correlates.

In this chapter we have suggested two ways in which the MMPI-A Content Scales can be used to help us understand adolescents' problems. First, the content scales are useful in refining interpretations of the empirically based clinical scales. In many instances, an elevation on a clinical scale is difficult to interpret because not all of the empirically established correlates apply for a particular test subject. Examination of content scale scores can help us eliminate correlates that are of low relevance for a particular test subject and focus on those that are more meaningful. Second, the MMPI-A Content Scales provide the bases for new hypotheses that cannot be made from the clinical scales. The content scales represent direct communication between the adolescent and the clinician and are presented in a sound psychometric framework. They allow clinicians to gain a unique perspective on adolescents' self-perceptions, an often difficult, yet highly critical, aspect of clinical assessment.

Although we are encouraged by our efforts to investigate the validity and usefulness of the MMPI-A Content Scales, we are aware that more research will be needed before we will know as much about interpreting these scales as we do about the clinical scales. We hope that this book will stimulate others to conduct additional studies with the MMPI-A Content Scales.

Appendixes

Biographical Information (Adolescent)

Subject # (Preassigned) _ _ _ _ _

Location # (Preassigned) _ _

Today's date _ _/_ _/_ _

Sex _____ Male _____ Female

Please provide the following information by checking the line by the item that applies to you.

1. What is your age?

   _____ 13
   _____ 14
   _____ 15
   _____ 16
   _____ 17
   _____ 18
   _____ 19
   _____ 20

2. What is your religion?

   Christian _____ Roman Catholic
   _____ Eastern Orthodox
   _____ Mormon
   _____ Protestant

   If Protestant, which denomination?

   _____

   _____ Jewish _____ Buddhist
   _____ Muslim _____ Baha'i
   _____ Hindu _____ None

3. What is your ethnic origin?

   _____ Asian _____ White
   _____ Black _____ Other
   _____ Hispanic
   _____ Native American

4. What is your present grade in school (or last grade completed, if not in school now)?

   _____ Seventh
   _____ Eighth
   _____ Ninth
   _____ Tenth
   _____ Eleventh
   _____ Twelfth

5. What marks do or did you usually get in school?

   _____ A's
   _____ B's
   _____ C's
   _____ D's
   _____ F's

6. What school activities do or did you participate in?

   Yes   No
   _____ _____ Sports
   _____ _____ Band/orchestra
   _____ _____ Clubs
   _____ _____ Drama
   _____ _____ Chorus
   _____ _____ Service
   _____ _____ Other

7. Which, if any, of these problems
   have you had in school?

   Yes   No
   _____ _____ Disciplinary/probation
   _____ _____ Suspension
   _____ _____ Expulsion
   _____ _____ Course failure
   _____ _____ Repeated grade

8. What are your plans when you are
   done with school?

   _____ Work/study program
   _____ Apprenticeship
   _____ Technical training
   _____ Four-year college
   _____ Two-year college
   _____ Commercial/business school
   _____ Trade school
   _____ Military service
   _____ Job
   _____ Undecided
   _____ Other

9. What is your father's education?

   _____ Grade school
   _____ Some high school
   _____ High-school graduate
   _____ Some college
   _____ College graduate
   _____ Graduate school

10. What is your mother's education?

    _____ Grade school
    _____ Some high school
    _____ High-school graduate
    _____ Some college
    _____ College graduate
    _____ Graduate school

11. What is (or was) your father's job?

    _____ President or other officer of a
    large company, lawyer,
    doctor, engineer, professor,
    architect
    _____ Business executive, engineer,
    teacher, social worker,
    optician, accountant, owner
    or manager of a large
    business, nurse
    _____ Bookkeeper, plant supervisor,
    salesperson, bank teller,
    secretary, photographer,
    owner or manager of small
    business or farm

_____ Assembly line worker, clerk,
welder, mechanic,
receptionist
_____ Factory laborer, custodian,
waiter
_____ Homemaker
_____ Unemployed
_____ Retired
_____ Other

12. What is (or was) your mother's job?

    _____ President or other officer of a
    large company, lawyer,
    doctor, engineer, professor,
    architect
    _____ Business executive, engineer,
    teacher, social worker,
    optician, accountant, owner
    or manager of a large
    business, nurse
    _____ Bookkeeper, plant supervisor,
    salesperson, bank teller,
    secretary, photographer,
    owner or manager of small
    business or farm
    _____ Assembly line worker, clerk,
    welder, mechanic,
    receptionist
    _____ Factory laborer, custodian,
    waitress
    _____ Homemaker
    _____ Unemployed
    _____ Retired
    _____ Other

13. How many sisters do you have?

    Number of   *Number of*
    Older   *Younger*

    _____   _____

14. How many brothers do you have?

    Number of   *Number of*
    Older   *Younger*

    _____   _____

15. If you are now living at home, do you
    live with (fill in all that apply)?

    Yes   No
    _____ _____ Father
    _____ _____ Mother
    _____ _____ Stepfather
    _____ _____ Stepmother
    _____ _____ Foster father
    _____ _____ Foster mother

_____ _____ Grandmother
_____ _____ Grandfather
_____ _____ Sister
_____ _____ Brother
_____ _____ Spouse
_____ _____ Son
_____ _____ Daughter
_____ _____ Aunts
_____ _____ Uncles

16. If you are living away from your family, do you live in a(n)?

_____ Apartment
_____ Barracks
_____ Dormitory
_____ Foster home
_____ Group home
_____ Rooming house
_____ Other

Life Events (Adolescent)

Subject # (Preassigned) _ _ _ _ _

Location # (Preassigned) _ _

Today's date _ _/_ _/_ _

Sex _____ Male _____ Female

Indicate by completing the yes (y) or no (n) circle if any of the events listed below have happened to you within the last six months. For each item answered yes, indicate whether the event had a negative effect, no effect or a positive effect on your life at the time it occurred.

		Yes	No	Negative Effect	No Effect	Positive Effect
1.	Change in schools	O	O	O	O	O
2.	Birth of brother or sister	O	O	O	O	O
3.	Brother or sister left home	O	O	O	O	O
4.	Mother or father lost job	O	O	O	O	O
5.	Mother or father left home	O	O	O	O	O
6.	Father's job changed, and he's away from home more	O	O	O	O	O
7.	Mother began working outside our home	O	O	O	O	O
8.	Separation or divorce of parents	O	O	O	O	O
9.	Marriage of mother or father to someone else	O	O	O	O	O
10.	Arrest of mother or father	O	O	O	O	O
11.	Arrest of sister or brother	O	O	O	O	O
12.	Mother or father sent to prison for one year or more	O	O	O	O	O
13.	Grandparent moved into our home	O	O	O	O	O
14.	Began junior high school	O	O	O	O	O
15.	Death of a grandparent	O	O	O	O	O

		Yes	No	Negative Effect	No Effect	Positive Effect
16.	Family earned much less money	O	O	O	O	O
17.	Discovered I was adopted	O	O	O	O	O
18.	Parents' arguments grew worse	O	O	O	O	O
19.	Death of father or mother	O	O	O	O	O
20.	Death of sister or brother	O	O	O	O	O
21.	Death of a close friend	O	O	O	O	O
22.	Family moved to a different house or apartment	O	O	O	O	O
23.	Had more serious disagreements with father or mother or both	O	O	O	O	O
24.	Parents married each other again or got back together	O	O	O	O	O
25.	Father or mother had an emotional problem requiring treatment	O	O	O	O	O
26.	Father or mother hospitalized for a serious illness	O	O	O	O	O
27.	Brother or sister hospitalized for a serious illness	O	O	O	O	O
28.	Referred to a counselor or therapist	O	O	O	O	O
29.	Started wearing glasses, braces, hearing aid, etc.	O	O	O	O	O
30.	Placed in a foster home	O	O	O	O	O
31.	Caught cheating or lying in school	O	O	O	O	O
32.	Dropped out of school or training program	O	O	O	O	O
33.	Got a driver's license	O	O	O	O	O
34.	Driver's license suspended	O	O	O	O	O
35.	Death of favorite family pet	O	O	O	O	O
36.	Had an abortion (if you are female), or girlfriend had an abortion (if you are male)	O	O	O	O	O
37.	Robbed or beaten up	O	O	O	O	O
38.	Sexually abused or raped	O	O	O	O	O
39.	Caught a venereal disease	O	O	O	O	O
40.	Had sex for the first time	O	O	O	O	O
41.	Had a gay sexual experience	O	O	O	O	O
42.	Stole something valuable	O	O	O	O	O

		Yes	No	Negative Effect	No Effect	Positive Effect
43.	Gained a lot of weight	O	O	O	O	O
44.	Lost a lot of weight	O	O	O	O	O
45.	Joined the military	O	O	O	O	O
46.	Had to appear in court	O	O	O	O	O
47.	Inherited a lot of money	O	O	O	O	O
48.	Had an accident that left scars	O	O	O	O	O
49.	Skipped a grade in school	O	O	O	O	O
50.	Became seriously ill and spent time in the hospital	O	O	O	O	O
51.	Held back a grade in school	O	O	O	O	O
52.	Placed on probation	O	O	O	O	O
53.	Was suspended from school	O	O	O	O	O
54.	Arrested for stealing	O	O	O	O	O
55.	Used drugs or alcohol	O	O	O	O	O
56.	Got pregnant (if you are female), or got girlfriend pregnant (if you are male)	O	O	O	O	O
57.	Became a member of a religious group	O	O	O	O	O
58.	Didn't make the team or other activity I tried out for	O	O	O	O	O
59.	Began going steady	O	O	O	O	O
60.	Broke up with my steady	O	O	O	O	O
61.	Began dating	O	O	O	O	O
62.	Got married	O	O	O	O	O
63.	Accepted by a college	O	O	O	O	O
64.	Started working part-time	O	O	O	O	O
65.	Got my first full-time job	O	O	O	O	O
66.	Lost my job	O	O	O	O	O
67.	Failed a major exam or course	O	O	O	O	O
68.	Joined a club or organization	O	O	O	O	O
69.	Elected an officer in an organization	O	O	O	O	O
70.	Treated differently by friends	O	O	O	O	O
71.	Unmarried sister got pregnant	O	O	O	O	O

	Yes	No	Negative Effect	No Effect	Positive Effect
72. Had an outstanding personal achievement (such as becoming head cheerleader, captain of a team, or making the National Honor Society)	O	O	O	O	O
73. Began senior high school	O	O	O	O	O
74. Won an outstanding prize or award	O	O	O	O	O

Record Review

1. Subject #   1. _ _ _ _ _   (1-5)

2. Location # (See Location Appendix)   2. _ _   (6-7)

3. Today's date   3. _ _/_ _/_ _   (8-13)

4. Admission date (If multiple admissions, use
   most *current* date)   4. _ _/_ _/_ _   (14-19)

5. School grade at admission (Not current school
   grade)   5. _ _   (20-21)

6. List DSM III diagnosis at admission (Code any   6.
   X's in the fifth digit as 0. Code any V's in the
   first digit as 0. If no diagnosis assigned, code
   79990. Fill in any remaining blanks with 99999.)

   a) _____   a) _ _ _ _ _   (22-26)

   b) _____   b) _ _ _ _ _   (27-31)

   c) _____   c) _ _ _ _ _   (32-36)

7. Current Problems—Include information
   presented by patient, parents, referral source or
   reported by treatment staff (0 = no; 1 = yes).

a.	Acting Out/Irresponsible Behavior	a. _____	(37)
b.	Anger Outbursts/Fighting	b. _____	(38)
c.	Oppositional Behavior	c. _____	(39)
d.	Running Away	d. _____	(40)
e.	Drug Use/Abuse	e. _____	(41)
f.	Impulsivity	f. _____	(42)
g.	Hyperactive Behavior/Overactivity	g. _____	(43)
h.	Social Withdrawal	h. _____	(44)
i.	Poor Social Skills	i. _____	(45)
j.	Identity Issues	j. _____	(46)
k.	Low Self-Esteem	k. _____	(47)
l.	Depression	l. _____	(48)
m.	Suicide Ideations/Gestures	m. _____	(49)
n.	Tension/Nervousness	n. _____	(50)
o.	Somatic Complaints	o. _____	(51)
p.	Truancy/School Avoidance	p. _____	(52)
q.	Academic Underachievement	q. _____	(53)
r.	Family Related Issues & Problems	r. _____	(54)

s.	Eating Problems	s. _____ (55)
t.	Bizarre Behavior	t. _____ (56)
u.	Bizarre Sensory Experiences	u. _____ (57)
v.	Bizarre Thought Processes/Delusions	v. _____ (58)
w.	Concentration Difficulties	w. _____ (59)
x.	Other	x. _____ (60)
y.	Other	y. _____ (61)
z.	Other	z. _____ (62)

8. Does the patient have a history of any of the following? (0 = no; 1 = yes)   8.

a. Being sexually active (e.g., evidence of sexual involvement with a boyfriend or girlfriend)   a. _____ (63)

b. Sexual acting out (e.g., multiple partners, prostitution, exhibitionism)   b. _____ (64)

c. Being sexually abused   c. _____ (65)

d. Being physically abused   d. _____ (66)

e. Gang involvement   e. _____ (67)

f. Assaultive behavior   f. _____ (68)

g. Having few or no friends   g. _____ (69)

9. If the patient has a history of suicide attempts, how many? If none, code 00.   9. _ _ (70-71)

10. Indicate the extent of the patient's experience with the following substances evident from chart:
(0 = definitely no use; 1 = some use; 2 = possible abuse; 3 = definite abuse; 9 = no information in chart)   10.

(See Drug Abuse Appendix for coding assistance)

a. Alcohol   a. _____ (72)

b. Amphetamines   b. _____ (73)

c. Barbiturates/Tranquilizers   c. _____ (74)

d. Cocaine   d. _____ (75)

e. Hallucinogens   e. _____ (76)

f. Inhalants   f. _____ (77)

g. Cannabis   g. _____ (78)

h. Narcotics   h. _____ (79)

i. Other _____   i. _____ (80)

11. Is there an indication of juvenile court involvement for a status offense(s)? (0 = no; 1 = yes)   11. _____ (1)

12. Is there an indication of court involvement for a non-violent, non-status offense(s) (e.g., stealing, breaking and entering)? (0 = no; 1 = yes)   12. _____ (2)

13. Is there an indication of court involvement for a violent non-status offense(s) (e.g., assault, rape, murder, armed robbery)? (0 = no; 1 = yes)   13. _____ (3)

14. Is there a history of learning disabilities? (0 = no; 1 = yes)   14. _____ (4)

15. If available, indicate intellectual level of patient. 15. _____ (5)

   1 = below average (IQ score below 80)
   2 = average (IQ score between 80-119 inclusive)
   3 = above average (IQ score greater than 119)
   9 = not available

16. Is there a record of previous psychiatric or psychological treatment of the patient? 16. _____ (6)

   0 = None
   1 = Evaluation only
   2 = Outpatient
   3 = Day Treatment
   4 = Inpatient
   5 = More than one type of the above

17. Is there a record of previous substance abuse treatment of the patient? 17. _____ (7)

   0 = None
   1 = Evaluation only
   2 = Outpatient
   3 = Day Treatment
   4 = Inpatient
   5 = More than one type of the above

18. Is there a record of a child protection worker being assigned to the child? (0 = no; 1 = yes) 18.

   a) _____ Presently   a) _____ (8)
   b) _____ In the past   b) _____ (9)

19. Is the patient on any of the following medications? List and see Drug Names Appendix for coding. (0 = no; 1 = yes) 19.

   a) Anti-Anxiety   a) _____ (10)
   b) Anti-Anxiety and Depression   b) _____ (11)
   c) Anti-Depressants   c) _____ (12)
   d) Anti-Psychotics   d) _____ (13)
   e) Hypnotics   e) _____ (14)
   f) Lithium   f) _____ (15)
   g) Medical Illness   g) _____ (16)
   h) Medical-Seizure   h) _____ (17)
   i) Medical-Side Effects   i) _____ (18)
   j) Ritalin and Other Stimulants   j) _____ (19)
      Uncertain (classify later)

20. Was the patient on any of the following medications in the past? List and see Drug Names Appendix for coding. (0 = no; 1 = yes) 20.

   a) Anti-Anxiety   a) _____ (20)
   b) Anti-Anxiety and Depression   b) _____ (21)
   c) Anti-Depressants   c) _____ (22)
   d) Anti-Psychotics   d) _____ (23)
   e) Hypnotics   e) _____ (24)
   f) Lithium   f) _____ (25)
   g) Medical Illness   g) _____ (26)

h) Medical-Seizure	h) _____	(27)
i) Medical-Side Effects	i) _____	(28)
j) Ritalin and Other Stimulants Uncertain (classify later)	j) _____	(29)

21. If the patient has a family history of any of the following, specify which relative.

21.

a) Substance Abuse	a) _____	(30)
b) Suicide	b) _____	(31)
c) Schizophrenia	c) _____	(32)
d) Affective Disorder	d) _____	(33)
e) Unknown Psychiatric	e) _____	(34)

0 = No history of this problem in chart
1 = Mother
2 = Father
3 = Sibling
4 = Other blood relative
5 = Both parents or parent and sibling
6 = Parent or sibling and at least one other blood relative
7 = More than one blood relative, but neither parent or sibling
8 = Family history indicated, but relative not specified
9 = Nonblood relative members of household

Discharge Information

22. If this sheet is not applicable, code a 0 and leave the rest blank. Otherwise, code a 1 and fill in completely.

22. _____   (35)

23. Date of discharge

23. _ _/_ _/_ _   (36-41)

24. Diagnoses at discharge

24.

a) _____   a) _ _ _-_ _   (42-46)

b) _____   b) _ _ _-_ _   (47-51)

c) _____   c) _ _ _-_ _   (52-56)

25. Was the patient discharged on any of the following medications?

25.

a) Anti-Anxiety	a) _____	(57)
b) Anti-Anxiety and Depression	b) _____	(58)
c) Anti-Depressants	c) _____	(59)
d) Anti-Psychotics	d) _____	(60)
e) Hypnotics	e) _____	(61)
f) Lithium	f) _____	(62)
g) Medical Illness	g) _____	(63)
h) Medical-Seizure	h) _____	(64)
i) Medical-Side Effects	i) _____	(65)
j) Ritalin and Other Stimulants Uncertain (classify later)	j) _____	(66)

26. Type of living arrangement at discharge:

26. _____   (67)

1 = Parental home
2 = Other relatives' home

        3 = Foster home
        4 = Other treatment facility
        5 = Independent living
        9 = No information

27.   Were any of the following recommended at discharge? (0 = no; 1 = yes)   27.

    a) Further assessment   a) _____   (68)
    b) More family involvement in therapy/family therapy   b) _____   (69)
    c) Other family member seek treatment   c) _____   (70)
    d) Outpatient psychiatric (psychological) therapy   d) _____   (71)
    e) Special school program   e) _____   (72)
    f) Inpatient psychiatric (psychological) treatment   f) _____   (73)
    g) Substance abuse treatment   g) _____   (74)
    h) Psychiatric day treatment   h) _____   (75)

28.   Status at discharge   28._____   (76)

    1. Completed treatment program
    2. Prematurely left treatment but had consent of treatment staff
    3. Terminated treatment program without consent of treatment staff (i.e., left against medical advice)

Item Composition of the MMPI-A Content Scales

A-anx (Adolescent-Anxiety)

MMPI-A Item Number*	Scoring Direction	Item
14	(T)	I work under a great deal of tension.
353	(T)	I have nightmares every few nights.
28	(T)	I find it hard to keep my mind on a task or job.
36	(T)	My sleep is fitful and disturbed.
134	(F)	Most nights I go to sleep without thoughts or ideas bothering me.
163	(T)	I am afraid of losing my mind.
185	(T)	I frequently find myself worrying about something.
196	(F)	I hardly ever notice my heart pounding and I am seldom short of breath.
209	(F)	I believe I am no more nervous than most others.
255	(T)	Life is a strain for me much of the time.
279	(T)	I cannot keep my mind on one thing.
281	(T)	I feel anxiety about something or someone almost all the time.
285	(T)	I have certainly had more than my share of things to worry about.
318	(T)	I have sometimes felt that difficulties were piling up so high that I could not overcome them.
375	(F)	I am usually calm and not easily upset.
377	(T)	I am apt to take disappointments so keenly that I can't put them out of my mind.
383	(T)	I worry quite a bit over possible misfortunes.
402	(T)	Several times a week I feel as if something dreadful is about to happen.
404	(T)	I sometimes feel that I am about to go to pieces.
424	(F)	I am not feeling much stress these days.
468	(T)	I often get confused and forget what I want to say.

A-obs (Adolescent-Obsessiveness)

52	(T)	I sometimes keep on at a thing until others lose their patience with me.
78	(T)	I do many things which I regret afterwards (I regret things more or more often than others seem to).
83	(T)	I have met problems so full of possibilities that I have been unable to make up my mind about them.
129	(T)	I have often lost out on things because I couldn't make up my mind soon enough.

185	(T)	I frequently find myself worrying about something.
310	(T)	I usually have to stop and think before I act even in small matters.
293	(T)	I have a habit of counting things that are not important such as bulbs on electric signs, and so forth.
307	(T)	Bad words, often terrible words, come into my mind and I cannot get rid of them.
308	(T)	Sometimes some unimportant thought will run through my mind and bother me for days.
368	(T)	I wish I could get over worrying about things I have said that may have injured other people's feelings.
370	(T)	My plans have frequently seemed so full of difficulties that I have had to give them up.
412	(T)	I have had periods in which I lost sleep over worry.
394	(T)	I must admit that I have at times been overly worried about something that really didn't matter.
421	(T)	I feel helpless when I have to make some important decisions.
444	(T)	It bothers me greatly to think of making changes in my life.

A-dep (Adolescent-Depression)

3	(F)	I wake up fresh and rested most mornings.
9	(F)	My daily life is full of things that keep me interested.
35	(T)	I have had periods of days, weeks, or months when I couldn't take care of things because I couldn't "get going."
49	(T)	I have not lived the right kind of life.
53	(T)	I wish I could be as happy as others seem to be.
62	(T)	Most of the time I feel blue.
68	(T)	These days I find it hard not to give up hope of amounting to something.
71	(F)	I usually feel that life is worthwhile.
88	(T)	I don't seem to care what happens to me.
91	(F)	I am happy most of the time.
124	(T)	I certainly feel useless at times.
139	(T)	I cry easily.
219	(T)	I believe I am a condemned person.
230	(T)	I believe my sins are unpardonable.
203	(T)	I brood a great deal.
242	(T)	No one cares much what happens to you.
259	(T)	Even when I am with people I feel lonely much of the time.
347	(T)	I am not happy with myself the way I am.
283	(T)	Most of the time I wish I were dead.
311	(T)	I am inclined to take things hard.
360	(F)	I very seldom have spells of the blues.
371	(T)	The future is too uncertain for a person to make serious plans.
372	(T)	Often, even though everything is going fine for me, I feel that I don't care about anything.
379	(T)	At times I think I am no good at all.
399	(T)	The future seems hopeless to me.
177	(T)	I sometimes think about killing myself.

A-hea (Adolescent-Health Concerns)

| 11 | (T) | There seems to be a lump in my throat much of the time. |

18	(F)	I am very seldom troubled by constipation.
17	(T)	I am troubled by attacks of nausea and vomiting.
25	(T)	I am bothered by an upset stomach several times a week.
470	(T)	I have a cough most of the time.
37	(T)	Much of the time my head seems to hurt all over.
41	(T)	Once a week or oftener I suddenly feel hot all over, for no real reason.
42	(F)	I am in just as good physical health as most of my friends.
44	(F)	I am almost never bothered by pains over my heart or in my chest.
50	(T)	Parts of my body often feel like they are burning, tingling, or "going to sleep."
54	(F)	I hardly ever feel pain in the back of my neck.
56	(T)	I am troubled by discomfort in the pit of my stomach every few days or oftener.
87	(F)	I have little or no trouble with my muscles twitching or jumping.
93	(T)	There seems to be a fullness in my head or nose most of the time.
97	(T)	Often I feel as if there is a tight band around my head.
106	(T)	I have a great deal of stomach trouble.
113	(F)	I have never vomited blood or coughed up blood.
112	(F)	I do not worry about catching diseases.
135	(F)	During the past few years I have been well most of the time.
138	(F)	I have never had a fit or convulsion.
143	(T)	The top of my head sometimes feels tender.
152	(F)	I have never had a fainting spell.
157	(F)	I seldom or never have dizzy spells.
193	(F)	My hearing is apparently as good as that of most people.
167	(T)	I feel weak all over much of the time.
168	(F)	I have very few headaches.
172	(F)	I have had no difficulty in keeping my balance in walking.
174	(F)	I do not have spells of hay fever or asthma.
210	(F)	I have few or no pains.
231	(T)	I have numbness in one or more places on my skin.
233	(F)	My eyesight is as good as it has been for years.
239	(F)	I do not often notice my ears ringing or buzzing.
275	(F)	I have never been paralyzed or had any unusual weakness of any of my muscles.
374	(F)	I have no trouble swallowing.
422	(T)	All my troubles would vanish if only my health were better.
187	(T)	I have a physical problem that keeps me from enjoying activities after school.
443	(T)	I have missed a lot of school in my life because of sickness.

A-aln (Adolescent-Alienation)

16	(T)	I am sure I get a raw deal from life.
20	(T)	No one seems to understand me.
39	(T)	If people had not had it in for me, I would be much more successful.
74	(F)	I am liked by most people who know me.
104	(F)	Anyone who is able and willing to work hard has a good chance of succeeding.

211	(T)	My way of doing things is apt to be misunderstood by others.
242	(T)	No one cares much what happens to you.
227	(T)	When in a group of people I have trouble thinking of the right things to talk about.
260	(F)	I get all the sympathy I should.
362	(T)	I don't like hearing other people give their opinions about life.
317	(T)	People often disappoint me.
369	(T)	I feel unable to tell anyone all about myself.
413	(T)	I could be happy living all alone in a cabin in the woods or mountains.
438	(T)	My parents do not understand me very well.
446	(T)	People are not very kind to me.
450	(F)	I get along with most people.
448	(F)	Most people think they can depend on me.
463	(T)	I have no close friends.
471	(T)	I avoid others to keep from being teased or tormented.
473	(T)	I don't seem to have as much fun as others my age.

A-biz (Adolescent-Bizarre Mentation)

22	(T)	Evil spirits possess me at times.
29	(T)	I have had very peculiar and strange experiences.
433	(T)	When I am with people, I am bothered by hearing very strange things.
250	(T)	My soul sometimes leaves my body.
92	(T)	I see things or animals or people around me that others do not see.
132	(T)	I believe I am being plotted against.
155	(T)	Someone has been trying to poison me.
173	(T)	There is something wrong with my mind.
439	(T)	I often hear voices without knowing where they come from.
428	(T)	There are persons who are trying to steal my thoughts and ideas.
315	(T)	Someone has control over my mind.
332	(T)	At one or more times in my life I felt that someone was making me do things by hypnotizing me.
278	(T)	Peculiar odors come to me at times.
291	(T)	I often feel as if things are not real.
296	(T)	I have strange and peculiar thoughts.
299	(T)	I hear strange things when I am alone.
314	(T)	People say insulting and vulgar things about me.
387	(F)	I have never seen a vision.
417	(T)	Ghosts or spirits can influence people for good or bad.

A-ang (Adolescent-Anger)

26	(T)	At times I feel like swearing.
34	(T)	At times I feel like smashing things.
111	(T)	Often I can't understand why I have been so irritable and grouchy.
128	(T)	At times I feel like picking a fist fight with someone.
201	(T)	I get mad easily and then get over it soon.
282	(T)	I easily become impatient with people.
367	(T)	I am often said to be hotheaded.
355	(F)	I am not easily angered.

378	(T)	I am often so annoyed when someone tries to get ahead of me in a line of people that I speak to that person about it.
382	(T)	I have at times had to be rough with people who were rude or annoying.
388	(T)	I am often sorry because I am so irritable and grouchy.
401	(T)	It makes me angry to have people hurry me.
416	(T)	I am very stubborn.
453	(T)	Others say I throw temper tantrums to get my way.
445	(T)	I often get into trouble for breaking or destroying things.
458	(T)	I sometimes get into fights when drinking.
461	(T)	I often have to yell to get my point across.

A-cyn (Adolescent-Cynicism)

47	(T)	I have often had to take orders from someone who did not know as much as I did.
55	(T)	I think a great many people exaggerate their misfortunes in order to gain the sympathy and help of others.
72	(T)	It takes a lot of argument to convince most people of the truth.
77	(T)	I think most people would lie to get ahead.
100	(T)	Most people are honest chiefly because they are afraid of being caught.
107	(T)	Most people will use somewhat unfair means to get what they want.
118	(T)	I often wonder what hidden reason another person may have for doing something nice for me.
211	(T)	My way of doing things is apt to be misunderstood by others.
213	(T)	I don't blame people for trying to grab everything they can get in this world.
225	(T)	It is safer to trust nobody.
238	(T)	Most people make friends because friends are likely to be useful to them.
263	(T)	A person who leaves valuable property unprotected is about as much to blame when it is stolen as the one who steals it.
265	(T)	I think nearly anyone would tell a lie to keep out of trouble.
267	(T)	Most people inwardly dislike putting themselves out to help other people.
295	(T)	I tend to be on my guard with people who are somewhat more friendly than I had expected.
371	(T)	The future is too uncertain for a person to make serious plans.
373	(T)	People have often misunderstood my intentions when I was trying to put them right and be helpful.
325	(T)	I have often met people who were supposed to be experts who were no better than I.
330	(T)	People generally demand more respect for their own rights than they are willing to allow for others.
334	(T)	I have often found people jealous of my good ideas, just because they had not thought of them first.
395	(T)	I have often worked for people who take credit for good work but who pass off mistakes on those who work for them.
406	(T)	A large number of people are guilty of bad sexual conduct.

A-con (Adolescent-Conduct Problems)

32	(T)	I sometimes steal things.
96	(F)	I have never done anything dangerous for the thrill of it.
99	(T)	I enjoy a race or game more when I bet on it.
117	(T)	If I could get into a movie without paying and be sure I was not seen, I would probably do it.
224	(T)	At times it has been impossible for me to keep from stealing or shoplifting something.
354	(T)	I can easily make other people afraid of me, and sometimes do for the fun of it.
232	(T)	I do not blame a person for taking advantage of people who leave themselves open to it.
234	(T)	At times I have been so entertained by the cleverness of some criminals that I have hoped they would get away with it.
356	(T)	I have done some bad things in the past that I never tell anybody about.
249	(F)	I have never been in trouble with the law.
252	(T)	If several people find themselves in trouble, the best thing for them to do is to agree upon a story and stick to it.
361	(T)	It is all right to get around the law if you don't actually break it.
391	(T)	When I am cornered I tell that portion of the truth which is not likely to hurt me.
442	(T)	People should always follow their beliefs even if it means bending the rules to do it.
445	(T)	I often get into trouble for breaking or destroying things.
455	(T)	I am often told that I do not show enough respect for people.
456	(T)	I like to shock people by swearing.
465	(F)	I don't like having to get "rough" with people.
345	(T)	My friends are often in trouble.
462	(T)	I often have to lie in order to get by.
469	(T)	Sometimes I do the opposite of what others want just to show them.
477	(T)	My friends often talk me into doing things I know are wrong.
478	(T)	I have done some bad things I didn't want to do because my friends thought I should.

A-lse (Adolescent-Low Self-Esteem)

74	(F)	I am liked by most people who know me.
58	(F)	I am an important person.
67	(T)	I am easily downed in an argument.
70	(T)	I am certainly lacking in self-confidence.
105	(F)	I seem to be about as capable and smart as most others around me.
124	(T)	I certainly feel useless at times.
358	(T)	I do not feel I can plan my own future.
384	(T)	It bothers me when people say nice things about me.
306	(T)	I have several times given up doing a thing because I thought too little of my ability.
379	(T)	At times I think I am no good at all.
385	(T)	I am apt to pass up something I want to do because others feel that I am not going about it in the right way.
415	(T)	I cannot do anything well.

400	(T)	People can pretty easily change my mind even when I have made a decision about something.
280	(T)	I am apt to pass up something I want to do when others feel that it isn't worth doing.
430	(T)	When problems need to be solved, I usually let other people take charge.
432	(T)	I recognize several faults in myself that I will not be able to change.
441	(T)	People do not find me attractive.
468	(T)	I often get confused and forget what I want to say.

A-las (Adolescent-Low Aspiration)

39	(T)	If people had not had it in for me, I would be much more successful.
170	(F)	I like to study and read about things that I am working at.
188	(F)	I like science.
351	(T)	The only interesting part of newspapers is the comic strips.
447	(F)	I usually expect to succeed in things I do.
218	(T)	I have difficulty in starting to do things.
324	(F)	If given the chance I could do some things that would be of great benefit to the world.
409	(F)	I like to read newspaper editorials.
411	(F)	I like to attend lectures on serious subjects.
340	(T)	I feel like giving up quickly when things go wrong.
397	(F)	I prefer work which requires close attention to work which allows me to be careless.
27	(T)	I shrink from facing a crisis or difficulty.
403	(F)	I like to read about science.
430	(T)	When problems need to be solved, I usually let other people take charge.
436	(F)	I want to go to college.
464	(T)	Others tell me that I am lazy.

A-sod (Adolescent-Social Discomfort)

43	(T)	I prefer to pass by people I know but have not seen for a long time, unless they speak to me first.
46	(F)	I am a very sociable person.
82	(F)	I like to go to parties and other affairs where there is lots of loud fun.
151	(T)	It makes me uncomfortable to put on a stunt at a party even when others are doing the same sort of things.
160	(T)	I find it hard to make talk when I meet new people.
178	(T)	I wish I were not so shy.
328	(T)	I am never happier than when alone.
248	(T)	I am likely not to speak to people until they speak to me.
262	(F)	I seem to make friends about as quickly as others do.
264	(T)	I dislike having people around me.
290	(T)	Often I cross the street in order not to meet someone I see.
316	(T)	At parties I am more likely to sit by myself or with just one other person than to join in with the crowd.
319	(F)	I love to go to dances.
331	(F)	I enjoy social gatherings just to be with people.
335	(F)	I enjoy the excitement of a crowd.
339	(F)	My worries seem to disappear when I get into a crowd of lively friends.
304	(T)	Whenever possible I avoid being in a crowd.

336	(F)	I do not mind meeting strangers.
245	(F)	In a group of people I would not be embarrassed to be called upon to start a discussion or give an opinion about something I know well.
292	(F)	I like parties and socials.
408	(T)	Some people think it's hard to get to know me.
410	(T)	I spend most of my spare time by myself.
450	(F)	I get along with most people.
475	(T)	I am usually very quiet around other people.

A-fam (Adolescent-Family Problems)

6	(F)	My father is a good man, or (if your father is dead) my father was a good man.
19	(T)	At times I have very much wanted to leave home.
86	(F)	I love my father, or (if your father is dead) I loved my father.
79	(F)	I have very few quarrels with members of my family.
119	(F)	I believe that my home life is as pleasant as that of most people I know.
137	(T)	I feel that I have often been punished without cause.
182	(F)	My mother is a good woman, or (if your mother is dead) my mother was a good woman.
181	(T)	My family treats me like a child.
184	(T)	There is very little love and companionship in my family as compared to other homes.
258	(F)	I love my mother, or (if your mother is dead) I loved my mother.
191	(T)	My parents often object to the kind of people I go around with.
194	(T)	Some of my family have habits that bother and annoy me very much.
269	(T)	My parents and family find more fault with me than they should.
352	(T)	I have reason for feeling jealous of one or more members of my family.
240	(T)	Once in a while I feel hate toward members of my family whom I usually love.
359	(T)	I get angry when my friends or family give me advice on how to live my life.
366	(T)	I have gotten many beatings.
302	(T)	The things that some of my family have done have frightened me.
277	(T)	My mother or father often make me obey even when I think it is unreasonable.
363	(T)	I often have serious disagreements with people who are close to me.
365	(F)	When things get really bad, I know I can count on my family for help.
303	(T)	Sometimes I enjoy hurting persons I love.
381	(T)	One or more members of my family are very nervous.
396	(T)	Some of my family have quick tempers.
398	(F)	The members of my family and my close relatives get along quite well.
405	(T)	I hate my whole family.
57	(T)	My parents do not like my friends.
438	(T)	My parents do not understand me very well.
344	(T)	I cannot wait for the day when I can leave home for good.

440	(T)	I have spent nights away from home when my parents did not know where I was.
215	(T)	My parents do not really love me.
451	(F)	We don't have trouble talking to each other in my family.
454	(T)	Others in my family seem to get more attention than I do.
457	(F)	I do the things I am supposed to do around home.
460	(F)	I have never run away from home.

A-sch (Adolescent-School Problems)

80	(T)	I have been suspended from school one or more times for bad behavior.
101	(T)	In school I have sometimes been sent to the principal for bad behavior.
153	(F)	I like school.
166	(F)	I can read a long while without tiring my eyes.
220	(T)	I am a slow learner in school.
257	(T)	In school I find it very hard to talk in front of the class.
380	(T)	Often I have not gone to school even when I should have.
389	(T)	In school my grades in classroom behavior (conduct) are quite regularly bad.
338	(T)	I can remember "playing sick" to get out of something.
12	(T)	My teachers have it in for me.
435	(T)	I would rather drive around with my friends than go to school activities or athletic events.
364	(T)	I am often upset by things that happen in school.
425	(T)	I think my teachers at school are stupid.
443	(T)	I have missed a lot of school in my life because of sickness.
69	(T)	I think school is a waste of time.
452	(T)	The only good thing about school is my friends.
459	(F)	My school grades are average or better.
464	(T)	Others tell me that I am lazy.
466	(T)	At school I am very often bored and sleepy.
33	(T)	I'm afraid to go to school.

A-trt (Adolescent-Negative Treatment Indicators)

20	(T)	No one seems to understand me.
88	(T)	I don't seem to care what happens to me.
242	(T)	No one cares much what happens to you.
356	(T)	I have done some bad things in the past that I never tell anybody about.
256	(T)	I am so touchy on some subjects that I can't talk about them.
357	(T)	It makes me nervous when people ask me personal questions.
358	(T)	I do not feel I can plan my own future.
369	(T)	I feel unable to tell anyone all about myself.
371	(T)	The future is too uncertain for a person to make serious plans.
414	(T)	I have one or more bad habits that are so strong it is no use fighting against them.
340	(T)	I feel like giving up quickly when things go wrong.
27	(T)	I shrink from facing a crisis or difficulty.
418	(T)	I am not responsible for the bad things that are happening to me.

421	(T)	I feel helpless when I have to make some important decisions.
419	(F)	My main goals in life are within my reach.
420	(T)	Mental illness is a sign of weakness.
423	(T)	I believe that people should keep personal problems to themselves.
426	(T)	Although I am not happy with my life, there is nothing I can do about it now.
444	(T)	It bothers me greatly to think of making changes in my life.
427	(T)	I hate to admit feeling sick.
434	(T)	I hate going to doctors even when I'm sick.
432	(T)	I recognize several faults in myself that I will not be able to change.
431	(F)	Talking over problems and worries with someone is often more helpful than taking drugs or medicine.
437	(F)	When I have a problem it helps to talk it over with someone.
449	(T)	I find it hard to break bad habits.
472	(T)	I have many secrets that I keep to myself.

References

Achenbach, T. M., & Edelbrock, C. S. (1978). The classification of child psychopathology: A review and analysis of empirical efforts. *Psychological Bulletin*, 85, 1275-1301.

Achenbach, T. M., & Edelbrock, C. S. (1983). *Manual for the Child Behavior Checklist and Revised Child Behavior Profile*. Burlington: University of Vermont, Department of Psychiatry.

Achenbach, T. M., & Edelbrock, C. S. (1986). *Manual for the Teacher's Report Form and the Teacher Version of the Child Behavior Checklist*. Burlington: University of Vermont, Department of Psychiatry.

Achenbach, T. M., & Edelbrock, C. S. (1987). *Manual for the Youth Self Report and Profile*. Burlington: University of Vermont, Department of Psychiatry.

Archer, R. P. (1984). Use of the MMPI with adolescents: A review of salient issues. *Clinical Psychology Review, 4,* 241-251.

Archer, R. P. (1987). *Using the MMPI with adolescents*. Hillsdale, NJ: Lawrence Erlbaum.

Archer, R. P., Gordon, R. A., Giannetti, R. A., & Singles, J. M. (1988). MMPI scale clinical correlates for adolescent inpatients. *Journal of Personality Assessment, 52,* 707-721.

Archer, R. P., White, J. L., & Orvin, G. H. (1979). MMPI characteristics and correlates among adolescent psychiatric inpatients. *Journal of Clinical Psychology, 35,* 498-504.

Ben-Porath, Y. S., & Butcher, J. N. (1989). Psychometric stability of rewritten MMPI items. *Journal of Personality Assessment, 53,* 645-653.

Ben-Porath, Y. S., Butcher, J. N., & Graham, J. R. (1991). Contribution of the MMPI-2 scales to the differential diagnosis of schizophrenia and major depression. *Psychological Assessment: A Journal of Consulting and Clinical Psychology*.

Ben-Porath, Y. S., & Williams, C. L. (1991, March). *Relationship of MMPI-A content to a psychiatric diagnostic interview*. Paper presented at the 26th Annual Symposium on Recent Developments in the Use of the MMPI (MMPI-2 and MMPI-A), St. Petersburg, FL.

Ben-Porath, Y. S., Williams, C. L., & Uchiyama, C. (1989). New scales for the Devereux Adolescent Behavior Rating Scale. *Psychological Assessment: A Journal of Consulting and Clinical Psychology, 1,* 58-60.

Bloom, B. L., Asher, S. J., & White, S. W. (1978). Marital disruption as a stressor: A review and analysis. *Psychological Bulletin, 85,* 867-894.

Burisch, M. (1984). Approaches to personality inventory construction. *American Psychologist, 39,* 214-227.

Butcher, J. N. (1965). Manifest aggression: MMPI correlates in normal boys. *Journal of Consulting Psychology, 29,* 446-455.

Butcher, J. N., Dahlstrom, W. G., Graham, J. R., Tellegen, A., & Kaemmer, B. (1989). *MMPI-2 (Minnesota Multiphasic Personality Inventory-2): Manual for administration and scoring.* Minneapolis: University of Minnesota Press.

Butcher, J. N., Graham, J. R., Williams, C. L., & Ben-Porath, Y. S. (1990). *Development and use of the MMPI-2 Content Scales.* Minneapolis: University of Minnesota Press.

Butcher, J. N., & Williams, C. L. (1992). *Essentials of MMPI-2 and MMPI-A interpretation.* Minneapolis: University of Minnesota Press.

Butcher, J. N., Williams, C. L., Graham, J. R., Archer, R. P., Tellegen, A., Ben-Porath, Y. S., & Kaemmer, B. (1992). *MMPI-A (Minnesota Multiphasic Personality Inventory-Adolescent): Manual for administration, scoring, and interpretation.* Minneapolis: University of Minnesota Press.

Chase, T. V., Chaffin, S., & Morrison, S. D. (1975). False positive adolescent MMPI profiles. *Adolescence, 40,* 507-519.

Coddington, R. D. (1972). The significance of life events as etiologic factors in the diseases of children: I. A survey of professional workers. *Journal of Psychosomatic Research, 16,* 7-18.

Colligan, R. C., & Offord, K. P. (1989). The aging MMPI: Contemporary norms for contemporary teenagers. *Mayo Clinic Proceedings, 64,* 3-27.

Costello, A., Edelbrock, C., Kalas, R., Kessler, M., & Klaric, S. A. (1983, October). *National Institute of Mental Health—Diagnostic Interview Schedule for Children (NIH—DISC).* Unpublished materials.

Cronbach, L. (1951). Coefficient alpha and the internal structure of tests. *Psychometrika, 16,* 297-334.

Dahlstrom, W. G., Welsh, G. S., & Dahlstrom, L. E. (1972). *An MMPI handbook: Vol. I. Clinical Interpretation* (rev. ed.). Minneapolis: University of Minnesota Press.

Dudley, H. K., Mason, M., & Hughes, R. (1972). The MMPI and adolescent patients in a state hospital. *Journal of Youth and Adolescence, 1,* 165-178.

Egeland, B., Erickson, M., Butcher, J. N., & Ben-Porath, Y. S. (1991). MMPI-2 profiles of women at risk for child abuse. *Journal of Personality Assessment, 57,* 254-263.

Ehrenworth, N. V., & Archer, R. P. (1985). A comparison of clinical accuracy ratings of interpretative approaches for adolescent MMPI responses. *Journal of Personality Assessment, 49,* 413-421.

Fleiss, J. L. (1971). Measuring nominal scale agreement among many raters. *Psychological Bulletin, 76,* 378-382.

Gallucci, N. T. (1987). The influence of elevated F-scales on the validity of adolescent MMPI profiles. *Journal of Personality Assessment, 51,* 133-139.

Gold, M., & Petronio, R. J. (1980). Delinquent behavior in adolescents. In J. Adelson (Ed.)., *Handbook of adolescent psychology* (pp. 495-535). New York: John Wiley.

Gottesman, I. I., Hanson, D. R., Kroeker, T. A., & Briggs, P. (1987). Appendix C: New MMPI normative data and power-transformed T-score tables for the Hathaway-Monachesi Minnesota cohort of 14,019 15-year-olds and 3,674 18-year-olds. In R. P. Archer, *Using the MMPI with adolescents* (pp. 241-297). Hillsdale, NJ: Lawrence Erlbaum.

Graham, J. R. (1977). *The MMPI: A practical guide.* New York: Oxford University Press.

Graham, J. R. (1987). *The MMPI: A practical guide* (2nd ed.). New York: Oxford University Press.

Graham, J. R. (1990). *MMPI-2: Assessing personality and psychopathology.* New York: Oxford University Press.

Greene, R. L. (1980). *The MMPI: An interpretive manual*. New York: Grune and Stratton.

Gutterman, E. M., O'Brien, J. D., & Young, J. G. (1987). Structured diagnostic interviews for children and adolescents: Current status and future directions. *Journal of the American Academy of Child and Adolescent Psychiatry, 26*, 621-630.

Hall, G. S. (1904). *Adolescence: Its psychology and its relations to physiology, anthropology, sociology, sex, crime, religion, and education* (Vols. 1-2). New York: D. Appleton.

Harris, R. E., & Lingoes, J. C. (1955, 1968). *Subscales for the MMPI: An aid to profile interpretation*. Unpublished manuscript, Langley Porter Neuropsychiatric Institute.

Hathaway, S. R., & McKinley, J. C. (1940). A multiphasic personality schedule (Minnesota): I. Construction of the schedule. *Journal of Psychology, 10*, 249-254.

Hathaway, S. R., & Monachesi, E. D. (1953). *Analyzing and predicting juvenile delinquency with the MMPI*. Minneapolis: University of Minnesota Press.

Hathaway, S. R., & Monachesi, E. D. (1957). The personalities of pre-delinquent boys. *Journal of Criminal Law, Criminology, and Political Science, 48*, 149-163.

Hathaway, S. R., & Monachesi, E. D. (1961). *An atlas of juvenile MMPI profiles*. Minneapolis: University of Minnesota Press.

Hathaway, S. R., & Monachesi, E. D. (1963). *Adolescent personality and behavior: MMPI patterns of normal, delinquent, drop-out, and other outcomes*. Minneapolis: University of Minnesota Press.

Hathaway, S. R., Monachesi, E. D., & Young, L. A. (1959). Rural-urban adolescent personality. *Rural Sociology, 24*, 331-346.

Hathaway, S. R., Monachesi, E. D., & Young, L. A. (1960). Delinquency rates and personality. *Journal of Criminal Law, Criminology, and Political Science, 50*, 433-440.

Hathaway, S. R., Reynolds, P. C., & Monachesi, E. D. (1969). Follow-up of the later careers and lives of 1,000 boys who dropped out of high school. *Journal of Consulting and Clinical Psychology, 33*, 370-380.

Herjanic, B., & Campbell, W. (1977). Differentiating psychiatrically disturbed children on the basis of a structured interview. *Journal of Abnormal Child Psychology, 5*, 127-134.

Herjanic, B., Herjanic, M., Brown, F., & Wheatt, T. (1975). Are children reliable reporters? *Journal of Abnormal Child Psychology, 3*, 41-48.

Herjanic, B., & Reich, W. (1982). Development of a structured psychiatric interview for children: Agreement between child and parent on individual symptoms. *Journal of Abnormal Child Psychology, 10*, 307-324.

Hjemboe, S., & Butcher, J. N. (1991). Couples in marital distress: A study of personality factors as measured by the MMPI-2. *Journal of Personality Assessment, 57*, 216-237.

Holden, R. R., & Fekken, G. C. (1990). Structured psychopathological test item characteristics and validity. *Psychological Assessment: A Journal of Consulting and Clinical Psychology, 2*, 35-40.

Kendall, P. C., & Williams, C. L. (1986). Therapy with adolescents: Treating the "Marginal Man." *Behavior Therapy, 17*, 522-537.

Klinefelter, D., Pancoast, D. L., Archer, R. P., & Pruitt, D. L. (1990). Recent adolescent MMPI norms: T-score elevation comparisons to Marks and Briggs. *Journal of Personality Assessment, 54*, 379-389.

Klinge, V., Culbert, J., & Piggott, L. R. (1982). Efficacy of psychiatric inpatient hospitalization for adolescents as measured by pre- and post-MMPI profiles. *Journal of Youth and Adolescence, 11*, 493-502.

Klinge, V., Lachar, D., Grisell, J., & Berman, W. (1978). Effects of scoring norms of adolescent psychiatric drug users' and non users' MMPI profiles. *Adolescence, 49*, 1-11.

Lachar, D. (1974). *The MMPI: Clinical assessment and automated interpretation.* Los Angeles: Western Psychological Services.

Lachar, D., & Alexander, R. S. (1978). Veridicality of self-report: Replicated correlates of the Wiggins MMPI content scales. *Journal of Consulting and Clinical Psychology, 42,* 267-273.

Lachar, D., Klinge, V., & Grisell, J. L. (1976). Relative accuracy of automated MMPI narratives generated from adult norm and adolescent norm profiles. *Journal of Consulting and Clinical Psychology, 44,* 20-24.

LeUnes, A., Evans, M., Karnei, B., & Lowry, N. (1980). Psychological tests used in research with adolescents, 1969-1973. *Adolescence, 15,* 417-421.

Lilienfeld, S. (1991). Assessment of psychopathy with the MMPI and MMPI-2. *MMPI-2 News & Profiles, 2,* 2.

Lipovsky, J. A., Finch, A. J., & Belter, R. W. (1989). Assessment of depression in adolescence: Objective and projective measures. *Journal of Personality Assessment, 53,* 449-458.

MacAndrew, C. (1965). The differentiation of male alcoholic outpatients from nonalcoholic psychiatric outpatients by means of the MMPI. *Quarterly Journal of Studies on Alcohol, 26,* 238-246.

MacAndrew, C. (1986). Toward the psychometric detection of substance misuse in young men: The SAP Scale. *Journal of Studies on Alcohol, 47,* 161-166.

Marks, P. A., Seeman, W., & Haller, D. L. (1974). *The actuarial use of the MMPI with adolescents and adults.* Baltimore: Williams and Wilkins.

Moore, D. D., & Handel, P. J. (1980). Adolescents' MMPI performance, cynicism, estrangement, and personal adjustment. *Journal of Clinical Psychology, 36,* 932-936.

Moore, R. H. (1984). The concurrent and construct validity of the MacAndrew Alcoholism Scale among at-risk adolescent males. *Journal of Clinical Psychology, 40,* 1264-1269.

Moore, R. H. (1985). Construct validity of the MacAndrew Scale: Secondary psychopathic and dysthymic-neurotic character orientations among adolescent male misdemeanor offenders. *Journal of Studies on Alcohol, 46,* 128-131.

Pancoast, D. L., & Archer, R. P. (1988). MMPI adolescent norms: Patterns and trends across four decades. *Journal of Personality Assessment, 52,* 691-706.

Spivack, G., Haimes, P. E., & Spotts, J. (1967). *Devereux Adolescent Behavior Rating Scale manual.* Devon, PA: Devereux Foundation.

Spivack, G., & Spotts, J. (1967). Adolescent symptomatology. *American Journal of Mental Deficiency, 72,* 74-95.

Tanner, J. M. (1971). Sequence, tempo, and individual variation in growth and development of boys and girls aged 12 to 16. *Daedalus, 100,* 907-930.

Tellegen, A., & Ben-Porath, Y.S. (in press). The new uniform T-scores for the MMPI-2: Rationale, derivation, and appraisal. *Psychological Assessment: A Journal of Consulting and Clinical Psychology.*

Walsh, S., Penk, W. E., Litz, B. T., Keane, T. M., Bitman, D., & Marx, B. (August, 1991). *Discriminant validity of the new MMPI-2 Content Scales.* Paper presented at the Ninety-ninth Annual Convention of the American Psychological Association, San Francicso.

Watson, N., Harris, W. G., Johnson, J. H., & LaBeck, L. (1983). MMPI clinical and content norms for a mixed psychiatric adolescent population. *Journal of Clinical Psychology, 39,* 696-709.

Wiggins, J. S. (1966). Substantive dimensions of self-report in the MMPI item pool. *Psychological Monographs, 80* (22, Whole No. 630).

Wiggins, J. S. (1969). Content dimensions in the MMPI. In J. N. Butcher (Ed.), *MMPI: Research developments and clinical applications.* New York: McGraw-Hill.

Wiggins, J. S., Goldberg, L., & Appelbaum, M. (1971). MMPI Content Scales: Interpretive norms and correlations with other scales. *Journal of Consulting and Clinical Psychology, 37,* 403-410.

Wiggins, J. S., & Vollmar, J. (1959). The content of the MMPI. *Journal of Clinical Psychology, 15,* 45-47.

Williams, C. L. (1986). MMPI profiles from adolescents: Interpretive strategies and treatment considerations. *Journal of Child and Adolescent Psychotherapy, 3,* 179-193.

Williams, C. L., Ben-Porath, Y. S., & Hevern, V. W. (1991, March). *Item level improvements for the MMPI-A.* Paper presented at the 26th Annual Symposium on Recent Developments in the Use of the MMPI (MMPI-2 and MMPI-A), St. Petersburg, FL.

Williams, C. L., Ben-Porath, Y. S., Uchiyama, C., Weed, N. C., & Archer, R. P. (1990). External validity of the new Devereux Adolescent Behavior Rating Scales. *Journal of Personality Assessment, 55,* 73-85.

Williams, C. L., Ben-Porath, Y. S., & Weed, N. C. (1990). Ratings of behavior problems in adolescents hospitalized for substance abuse. *Journal of Adolescent Chemical Dependency, 1,* 95-112.

Williams, C. L., & Butcher, J. N. (1989a). An MMPI study of adolescents: I. Empirical validity of the standard scales. *Psychological Assessment: A Journal of Consulting and Clinical Psychology, 1,* 251-259.

Williams, C. L., & Butcher, J. N. (1989b). An MMPI study of adolescents: II. Verification and limitations of code type classifications. *Psychological Assessment: A Journal of Consulting and Clinical Psychology, 1,* 260-265.

Williams, C. L., Butcher, J. N., & Graham, J. R. (1986, March). *Appropriate MMPI norms for adolescents: An old problem revisited.* Paper presented at the 21st Annual Symposium on Recent Developments in the Use of the MMPI, Clearwater, FL.

Williams, C. L., Hearn, M. D., Hostetler, K., & Ben-Porath, Y. S. (1991). *A comparison of several epidemiological measures for adolescents: MMPI, DISC, and YSR.* Unpublished manuscript.

Wirt, R. D., & Briggs, P. F. (1959). Personality and environmental factors in the development of delinquency. *Psychological Monographs, 73* (Whole No. 485), 1-47.

Wisniewski, N. M., Glenwick, D. S., & Graham, J. R. (1985). MacAndrew Scale and sociodemographic correlates of adolescent alcohol and drug abuse. *Addictive Behaviors, 10,* 55-67.

Wolfson, K. P., & Erbaugh, S. E. (1984). Adolescent responses to the MacAndrew Alcoholism Scale. *Journal of Consulting and Clinical Psychology, 52,* 625-630.

Index

Carolyn L. Williams is associate professor of epidemiology in the School of Public Health, University of Minnesota, coauthor, with James N. Butcher, John R. Graham, and Yossef S. Ben-Porath, of *Development and Use of the MMPI-2 Content Scales* (Minnesota, 1990), and coauthor of *MMPI-A: Manual for Administration, Scoring, and Interpretation* (Minnesota, 1992). Her work also includes several books and articles on refugee mental health. The most recent is *Mental Health Services for Refugees* (1991), coedited with Joseph Westermeyer and Ahn Nga Nguyen.

James N. Butcher is professor of psychology at the University of Minnesota. He is author of numerous articles and books on the MMPI, including *MMPI-2 in Psychological Treatment* (1990). He is a coauthor of the MMPI-A manual and coauthor with Carolyn L. Williams of *Essentials of MMPI-2 and MMPI-A Interpretation* (Minnesota, 1992). Butcher is editor of the American Psychological Association's journal *Psychological Assessment*.

Yossef S. Ben-Porath is assistant professor of psychology at Kent State University. His articles on the MMPI-2 have appeared in *Psychological Assessment* and the *Journal of Personality Assessment*. He is coauthor of *Development and Use of the MMPI-2 Content Scales* and of the MMPI-A manual, and a codeveloper of several MMPI-2 and MMPI-A scales. Dr. Ben-Porath is also a frequent presenter at MMPI-2 and MMPI-A workshops.

John R. Graham is professor of psychology at Kent State University. He has contributed extensively to the research literature concerning the MMPI/MMPI-2. He is author of *MMPI-2: Assessing Personality and Psychopathology* (1990) and coauthor of *Development and Use of the MMPI-2 Content Scales* (Minnesota, 1990), the MMPI-A manual, and *Psychological Testing* (1984).